An Introduction to

Collaboration, Teamwork, and *NETWORKING*:

A Case for Working Together Systematically to
Achieve Successful Living

2nd Edition

By
Gerald A. Higginbotham
and
Joyce M. Coleman

Locust Hill Publishing
St. Louis, MO
www.locusthillpublishing.com

Moments of Contemplation

The key to an effective life is to be principle, purpose, process and value driven.
Dr. Gerald's Teachings

An Introduction to

Collaboration, Teamwork, and *NETWORKING*:

A Case for Working Together Systematically to
Achieve Successful Living

2nd Edition

By
Gerald A. Higginbotham
and
Joyce M. Coleman

ISBN: 978-0970091833

Printed in the United States of America

Published by Locust Hill Publishing
www.locusthillpublishing.com

Contents

What others are saying about this book

By promoting Prosumerism in their book *Collaboration, Teamwork and Networking*, Gerald Higginbotham and Joyce Coleman promote a profoundly fascinating concept. It is the concept that consumers cooperatively and collaboratively produce and manage the production and distribution of the very goods and services that they consume. By doing so, consumers therefore build wealth and develop assets in the communities in which they reside. This is a positive prescription to save our country from the recent near-collapse of our economy, by providing the means to rebuild our communities that were devastated by it.

Rev. Tony E. Pierce
Co-Senior Pastor, Heaven's View Christian Fellowship
Co-Founder, Community Development & Service Collaboration
Co-Founder, Community Development & Service Institute
Peoria, IL

Brother Gerald is direct and writes boldly and honestly even about systems problems within our African American churches. However, he spends the most time on meaningful solutions. Any minister or active layman that reads Brother Gerald's books will be better able to teach about spiritually based economics and social changes. He writes like Paul told us to communicate: Tell the truth, but in love. He does.

Dr. C.T. Vivian
Civil Rights Activist, Author & Speaker

[Collaboration, Teamwork, and Networking] suggests that business as usual won't make the grade and that energies and resources are most powerful when consolidated through collaboration. [The book] presents thoughtful and pragmatic blueprints for those who want to maximize their leverage, resources, and opportunities. Finally, this book is the stuff of meaningful 21st Century empowerment, networking for a collective cause.

Attorney Donald M. Temple
Civil Rights Lawyer
Howard University Alumnus, Washington, D.C.

Collaboration, Teamwork and Networking is an insightful and impactful view of the path to success for our people, providing an achievable framework for living more abundantly. [The book] emphasizes the importance of our political involvement, as well as taking a proactive stance concerning health in our communities - issues that are paramount to our very survival. Finally, the glimpse Dr. Gerald gives us in "The New Society" fills us with hope - not merely for surviving the Information Age, but being truly successful and preparing future generations to take a rightful place in "The New Society". Thank you Dr. Gerald for your vision!

David Rice
DL Rice Investments, Los Angeles

I couldn't put the book down. I wanted to find out what else we need to do to change the communities of the world... This book is a thought-provoking look at what the future could be if we strive for a better life, existence. [It] draws you in to what is, what could be and what we need to do to reach the "what could be." What a guidebook to help change our lives, our families lives, society and the world. Societies change after reading books such as this one.

William Heckel
Principal Brown Elementary School, Hazelwood, MO

What a wakeup call for folks that would want to change their lives and make a difference in their lives. Fantastic info and direction.....

Bruce Breckle
Trainer, Boeing Aircraft

It shakes off the chains of ignorance and catapults you to success through the unity of our collective minds and actions. Quite a masterpiece!

Tony Hamilton
IT Consultant, AT&T

If only I had read *Collaboration, Teamwork, and Networking* when it was first published! This book fully predicted the perfect storm of a society out of balance that would create an economic meltdown, health catastrophe, and political upheaval. We experienced that upheaval during the last couple of years. I am now paying very close attention to the solutions outlined, and will be working to help implement them. I hope others will follow suit.

Rev. Vickie Caldwell
St. Louis Metropolitan Clergy Coalition

How do I put into words what the Success-Networking experience has meant in my life? I am among that incredibly large percentage of African American males that have been incarcerated. Through the system developed by Dr. Gerald, and put in place in East St. Louis, I am now employed in a position of respect and responsibility. This has been my lifeline, an opportunity to live again. I hope and I pray that others will adopt this process, one that permits giving a second chance to people like me.

Carl Kimmins
Manager, Soul Food Café, East St. Louis

This writing serves as a great primer for understanding the possibilities of defying the economic climate and producing life changing outcomes that can dramatically impact communities. There is a careful defining of the challenge and a described alternative that can be modeled when put into practice. It will require a commitment, but doesn't everything that has long lasting impact?

Douglass Petty, Ph.D.
Pastor, Author, Organizational Consultant, Life Coach
St. Louis

Collaboration, Teamwork, and Networking provides practical "how to" information that helps us to move from teaching and preaching to doing. Those of us who are blessed to minister to congregations have a unique opportunity to help our people embrace the marvelous potential that lies within. The material that is presented in the book prepares our people for excellence, to become leaders of positive change. We have an opportunity to help them become the change they wish to see. The system that this book teaches will help us usher in that change.

Rev. Sammie Jones
Pastor, Mt. Zion Baptist Church – St. Louis
Board Chair, St. Louis Black Leadership Roundtable

… Extraordinarily progressive, economic stimulus development plan for community sustainability ever promoted… Bold concept.

Deborah Hopkins
Certified Travel Agent/Owner

Buy the book! It will be a life changer for you as it has been and is continuing to be for our congregation. This 2nd edition of *Teamwork, Collaboration, and Networking* builds on what I learned in the first book. It shows me exactly how to implement systems that the first book described. What is exciting for our congregation is to actually put the words to action as we integrate the Mind Renewal module into our learning. It is helping our group embrace their potential, individually and collectively. I don't believe I could ask for anything more.

Juliette Hite
Pastor, Total Praise and Worship Center, St. Louis

Moments of Contemplation

Lack of knowledge causes destruction, but incorrect
information keeps you in bondage.
Dr. Gerald's Teachings

ACKNOWLEDGEMENTS

How do you say thank you to so many people who have touched your life in so many wonderful ways? Although daunting, we will try.

Let us begin with an acknowledgement of our families. Dr. Gerald's caring, supportive and loving wife, Marcia and two sons, Gerald II and Kaleb, allowed the time to make this book a reality.

His mother, Minnie Higginbotham, deposited in him the desire to play until you win, and all his wonderful brothers, sisters, nieces and nephews have been so supportive throughout the years.

Joyce's husband, John, brings tolerance, an understanding of the human condition, and support. Sister and friend Elsie is always there to provide whatever is needed, and is the link to a much-loved brother and extended family. This kind of support permits creativity and space, and is much appreciated.

Our mentors and colleagues gave and continue to give so much. Dr. Gerald's list is exhaustive. Ernest Lindo came along at the right time in his life and planted a process in him that has been evolving ever since. Thank you Dr. Fred Price, Dr. C.T. Vivian, Dr. Claude Anderson, George Fraser, Dr. I.V.

Hilliard, Pastor Bill Winston, Pastor Alfred Harvey, Pastor Charles Roberson, and Pastor John Chaney for their time and all the wisdom and knowledge they shared with him. Thank you to the early Success Networking members: Melanie Barton, Eugene Bosley, Beachum Buchanan, Bonnie Caldwell, Robert Cole, Eddie Davis, Kim Douglas, Jose' Fleming, Juliette Hite, Madeline Long, Keith McGull, Nancy Montgomery, Frank Morris, Marcelle Rhone, Theresa Robinson, Arthur Porter, Stephanie Turner, Bobbie Willis, Gary Waugh, and Darryl Worth. We especially thank the team that tested our model at two East St. Louis, Missouri businesses: Roxanne Alexander, Marlon Brown, Tony Bush, Graci Hope, Aubrey Keller, Carl Kimmins, Harold Parker, Timothy Stewart, Antwon Strong, Sue Thomas, and Tiffany Williams. We acknowledge, and express thanks for, the incredible support provided by the city of East St. Louis, including Mayor Alvin Parks. Joyce's mentors are the numerous people in her professional and private network who are always there. Their knowledge and skill sets are so vast that, if set in focused motion, could alter the course of a planet.

Marcia Higginbotham has provided an amazing service of reviewing every word in this document and offering her comments. She saw everything from the vantage point of the reader – you. Rarely have we seen anyone with such dedication, eye for detail, and commitment to a project. Thank you, Marcia, many times over.

The most important thank you goes to our God and Lord and Savior Jesus Christ. Although we choose different ways to express our beliefs, both of us understand the source of Life and Blessings.

Last, but not least, thank you - the reader - for making a decision to purchase and read this book. It will inspire you to go to the next level.

Moments of Contemplation

I will make thy seed as the dust of the earth: so that if a man can number the dust of the earth, then shall thy seed also be numbered.

God to Abraham
Genesis 13:16

FOREWORD

Networking works when you fully understand that there is inherent value in every human being and every human relationship regardless of title or position. Only when we mature enough to stop prejudging people as to their worthiness of our assistance can we truly give without expectation. When you give without expectation, you are networking FOR THE BENEFIT OF OTHERS, and therefore the law of increasing returns will reward you tenfold. There are no exceptions to this law. Had the people in my life prejudged me because I lived in publicly subsidized tenement housing or because I mopped floors at LaGuardia Airport, I would never have had the assistance I needed to fully blossom and maximize my full human potential. At some point neither would most people. This is the spiritual and philosophical underpinning of effective networking.

Networking works when you understand that there is very little that you can do or have in life without working with other people. Therefore, you work diligently on building and developing your infrastructure of human resources by finding a way to add value.

Networking works when you understand that the whole is greater than the sum of its parts. Networks must be built upon a foundation of established relationships, first of all, but they can extend beyond. Building that essential foundation, however, takes time. You must have an established rapport with your key core of networking contacts.

Perhaps most important to making networking work is showing appreciation for the contributions of your fellow networkers. Remember how your mother labored to ingrain gratitude in you? ("Now, say 'Thank You.'") Well, as usual, your mother knew best. Expressing gratitude is positive reinforcement. It works. I make a point to thank people just for making a call for me or sending me some special article they think I might be interested in. All of this takes time, but it is time invested toward a larger reward.

This book fully explores the breath of rewards we receive from the morally grounded and spiritually rooted principles of collaborations, teamwork and networking. Thank you Gerald and Joyce for helping everyone understand clearly that "it takes teamwork to make the dream work."

George Fraser
Speaker, Author; *Success Runs In Our Race: The Complete Guide to Effective Networking in Black America* (www.frasernet.com)

A Message from the Authors:

Dear Reader,

This 2nd edition of *Collaboration, Teamwork, and Networking* contains all the material of our original book, plus insights we gleaned from our experiences in the trenches. This edition delves more deeply into the requirements and components of our success-networking system than our previous edition.

The success-networking process is built on the framework of Cooperative Economics, which is not a new concept. However, we expand the concept to include social systems, and we suggest a more robust participation in the political process. The book is aimed at providing a snapshot of how the existing economic, political, and social systems favor the status quo. We tried to paint a word picture of what the status quo looks and feels like in many of our nation's urban communities. Our aim is to show that inactivity and denial are not options. The book offers a framework for people and organizations to be proactive in combining their resources to create businesses that produce jobs and other services that help communities to thrive.

This second edition provides plain talk about what really happens when you introduce a new vision of what could be, one that is readily attainable. It addresses how fear of change, even change for the better, can hold people hostage. This fear of change is beyond economic status, beyond gender. It is a human condition. However, it can be overcome. In this book we offer insights on how to overcome the fear that keeps us locked in situations that are not good for us, nor are they good for our families and communities.

Our ongoing collaboration to write about how we can work together to achieve what we cannot achieve as a single entity represents an exercise in exactly what we write about in the book. We bring different skill sets, experiences, and perspectives to the project. One of us is rooted in a biblical, spiritual, and activist perspective; the other from a people, process and systems environment. However, we both agree on a vision for change, a need for change, and that people are more than up to the task of making change happen. We also agree that mind, body, and spirit must be integrated in order for positive, sustainable change to happen. We both believe that all things are possible through Christ who strengthens us.

Since our first book was released, the world we predicted has become a reality. The need for change is more compelling than ever. Economic circumstances and their global impact have demonstrated that it is no longer wise or safe to be dependent upon "somebody else" for jobs, wealth, political influence, or desirable communities in which to live. The time is right now to initiate practices based on shared vision, goals and wealth-building.

We saw firsthand the impact of resistance to change, and the issue of trust.

Change is hard. The familiar is comforting, even when uncomfortable. If one is advocating change, the benefits of change must clearly outweigh the loss of comfort factor. Those benefits must be seen in vivid color, and understood on a visceral level.

Although we already knew theoretically that trust must be earned, our experiences demonstrated that it's more complicated than that. Therefore, in this issue we address practical ways to begin and nurture environments conducive to trust.

Our forefathers had a more compelling impetus for working together than our generation. It was clear to them that life and liberty were at stake. Now, that clarity of understanding is muddied. We perceive that there is a less compelling case for working together because there is an illusion of safety. However, our perception is sadly flawed. Today, just as it was for our forefathers, it is critical that we find common ground around which we can unite. Our very lives depend on it.

Sadly, we must admit that this 2nd edition of *Collaboration, Teamwork, and Networking* only scratches the surface of issues that should compel change, and actions needed to facilitate that change. However, we must begin somewhere. That *somewhere* has already been initiated by others, and we are only a small part of the process. What we do know is the process we recommend is based upon an age-old practice of working together to achieve a common vision that has, unfortunately, fallen by the wayside over decades. We've taken the age-old practice of collaboration, teamwork, and networking and through focus and systems created a new dynamic that addresses many 21st century issues that threaten our security and survival.

Enjoy and be blessed.

Gerald A. Higginbotham (Dr. Gerald)
Joyce M. Coleman

Moments of Contemplation

Wisdom is one of the most important things on the Earth; it is the key to life.
Dr. Gerald's Teaching

Wisdom is the principle thing; therefore get wisdom: and with all thy getting get understanding.
Proverbs 4:7

INTRODUCTION

In the 1st edition of *Collaboration, Teamwork, and Networking,* we introduced you to the concept of success-networking by describing an aspirational model of a success community. The potential for that kind of community still exists, but getting there is a journey.

For the past four years we have shared the success-networking concept with numerous groups in urban communities throughout the United States. While our participants could see the value immediately, much time was spent explaining the concept.

The 2nd edition of our book demonstrates that success-networking is a tried and true process that a community can use to develop and maintain the economic, social, and political environment it wishes to enjoy. Although the process outlined in this book may differ slightly from other models, the premise is the same. It is a vehicle that permits people to unite within a carefully crafted system for the purpose of creating financial security, wellness, and other institutions that provide the environment they wish for themselves and their families. Strategic business creation is the system's driver.

Networking was a natural choice for many of our African-American forefathers. People in urban and rural communities banded together to ensure that its members had food, shelter, and places to educate their children. They used what they produced. They may not have thought of themselves as entrepreneurs, and they may have bartered their goods and services, but many produced what they consumed. Without ready access to transportation, and because many [African-Americans] were locked out of participation in mainstream society, their issue was survival. African American churches were instrumental in these efforts, as it was the one place that was consistently accessible as a gathering spot. Legal and cultural changes led to greater freedom of movement and access to more of society's mainstream systems. Ever changing global communication networks and availability of travel to any place on the globe radically changed the landscape. The tools and practices of our forefathers became obsolete. Our churches became self-focused. However, we believe that the premise of community initiatives in the development of economic, social, and political power is as valid as ever. Given the state of many of our urban communities, it is critical that we return to community-led initiatives that lead to the development of small businesses and a sense of community ownership.

Examples of more recent success-networking projects are numerous. The Mondragon Corporation is the world leader in the Co-operative movement. According to information on its website, it has developed worker-owned businesses in 17 countries. A review of its Corporate Management Model provides insights into its success.

Is it possible for people throughout communities in the United States to develop the kind of community that we are describing? Absolutely! Clearly, the need exists. It has been accomplished by others. Our churches and other organizations already have networks of people that can easily re-set and expand their goals to include a success-networking community model that includes business creation. The capabilities are in our genes, passed down from our forefathers who worked magic out of scant resources.

Life is choice-driven. The quality of life that you live is based upon the quality of decisions you make. But, if you have not been given all the right information, how can you make the right choices? This book helps you discover that life is lived on various levels that come at different stages in one's life. Most people spend far too long at the crossroads of life, waiting and expecting to go to a higher level without understanding the process and actions required to get there. In order to advance to the next level, one of the following has to take place: *You will have to gain something, give up something, or trade something.*

Let's assume that you have just come to a fork in the road. You have been advised that one road leads to failure, i.e., sickness, poverty, and destruction. You have also been advised that the other road leads to prosperity, i.e. freedom, wellness, financial security, and empowerment. Let's call this choice *The More Abundant Life*. Which road would you take? For most the choice is quite simple; you would select the road to *The More Abundant Life*.

However, there is a problem. There are no signs on the roads, so there is no way of knowing which road leads where. So how do you decide which road to take? At this point some people would give up and do nothing, accepting failure. Some people would choose aimlessly, with a high risk of failure. And, some people, recognizing the importance of the decision and the need for more information would begin a process of investigation. If you're reading this, you are in the third group of people, i.e. those seeking more information.

Just off the roadside stands a person who has all of the information you need to make the right choice. You approach the person at the side of the road and he tells you that the road to the abundant life is on the right. However, he also tells you that the abundant life that you seek is part of the New Society. It's called the *Information Society,* and in order to get past the tollgate you must do two things. First, you must endeavor to learn about the health and economic systems that support and sustain the abundant life. Second, you must adopt an attitude of learning, caring, and sharing. You see, in the New Society, true abundance can only be accomplished through collaborations, and networks of caring and sharing.

Let's look at it another way.

What if there was **somewhere** you could go, right in your own neighborhood, wherever you live in the world, where there are people who share your desire for abundant living, people who will help you and expect nothing in return?

What if there was **somewhere** you'd never have to be alone, where there was always someone who would understand, without judgment, because they share your most basic dream?

What if there was **somewhere** you could grow as a person, a parent, a spouse, a friend, a contributor to your community – where you'd feel alive, useful, and empowered while you helped others to grow?

What if there was *somewhere* you could go, every day, where only people who sincerely desire to build their personal foundation, financial worth, and relationships were gathered?

What if there was *somewhere* you could go, every day, where only people who want to build up their community, create jobs for all who want them, have a positive impact on the community's politics, and leave a legacy for their children were gathered?

What if there was *somewhere* you could learn the simple secrets that allow success, happiness and abundance to flow into your life?

Well, would you go there? Congratulations! You have just begun your journey by picking up this book.

We make no claims of having a magic bullet that will instantly make all the wonderful situations described above immediately available. It is unreasonable to expect an instant fix to structural flaws that have been in place for decades. However, this we do know. The changes we advocate are part of a journey; they are achievable over time, given the appropriate tools and focus. We have already begun to experience the impact of what we propose, some of which is shared in *Lessons Learned*, Section VII.

Your journey to the life you desire and deserve requires a *mindset* that continuously embraces and evaluates new information. It requires continuously learning, and unlearning information and habits that are not constructive. So, before you begin your journey, we want you to be prepared.

Moments of Contemplation

Give instruction to a wise man, and he will be still wiser; teach a just man, and he will increase in learning.
Proverbs 9:9

My people are destroyed for a lack of knowledge; because thou hast rejected knowledge.
Hosea 4:6a

Ignorance must be overcome through knowledge and learning.
Dr. Gerald's Teachings

SECTION I:
LEARNING: CORNERSTONE OF A SUCCESS PROJECT

Preparation for Success

In the 1st edition of *Collaboration, Teamwork, and Networking,* we provided five components to what we call The Laws of Learning: **Information; Repetition; Role Model/Example; Pattern/Plan; Practice; and Mastery and Skill.** While those laws are just as relevant today as when we wrote about them, we discovered that in order for understanding to take place, more than theoretical information about the learning process is required. We saw firsthand that information and exercises that connect learners to results were critical to the overall success of the project.

Why is learning important to working together to achieve successful outcomes? Let's begin with the "successful" qualification. "Success" implies that the results of your efforts will yield exactly what you had in mind, or will exceed what you had in mind. Successful activity produces desired results.

Our "in-the-trenches" experiences demonstrated that strategic learning is as critical to a venture's success as any other business element. Strategic learning that supports success-networking includes everything people need to work together successfully in pursuit of a common vision.

Imagine that you and your best friends decide to work together to open up a business, such as a day care center for senior citizens. One person in the group has experience in this arena as a financial manager. Others have various work experiences, but nothing related to day care centers for senior citizens. Can you imagine the group proceeding with this exercise before engaging in some serious learning exercises? For instance, do members in your group know the answers to the following questions?

1. What are the critical components of this business?

2. Who are the potential customers and how can they be reached?

3. What are the customer needs, in their own words?

4. What is the role of each of the friends who are developing this business?

5. Does each member of the group have a clear vision of what they are trying to accomplish?

6. Is each passionate about the impact of the project's results?

7. How will you measure success?

8. What are similar businesses that are successful doing?

9. How can your group do it better?

10. How can the group set aside egos (particularly the ego of the person who floated the idea, or put up money for the project) and concentrate on the best actions for the business?

11. How do you maintain harmony, even amid different opinions, so that each project participant actually enjoys the journey?

We also discovered that people who have a well-developed sense of self-esteem contribute more openly and thoughtfully. They are less likely to feel intimidated or hoard information. They are less likely to feel threatened by new ideas, and don't mind vigorous discussion. This characteristic was so important to a positive work environment that we incorporated a training module to address the issue of "knowing oneself."

While readers may say to themselves that they don't have to worry because they have no intention of opening a day care center for senior citizens, the same series of check points apply if you want to achieve the results you promised to your organization or other supporters. If you haven't achieved your desired results with your projects, ask yourself what do *you* need to learn and/or unlearn in order to experience success.

How do other organizations that advocate working collaboratively and interdependently handle learning? The most successful business cooperative in the world has already established that strategic education is the key foundational piece to success. Simply put, this organization ensures that its people are properly trained to become successful participants in their systems. Our own experience confirms the wisdom of that choice.

Based upon lessons we learned, along with what others who have blazed trails in the area of working collaboratively and interdependently offer, we concluded that strategic learning is critical to making sure that a group is ready to take on a project. We recommend that any organization that plans to initiate a success-networking project (or any other project) ensure that all participants are well trained. The learning that we recommend is more broad-based than simply acquiring skills to perform a task. Learning must encompass how to create and sustain the desired spirit of the organization. Success depends on it.

Following are key areas where knowledge, skill, and behaviors are critical to success.

1. We discovered the hard way that it is foolish to attempt to implement any social or business model without providing great clarity about the model's objectives and processes, and the roles of its participants. Whether the product is a restaurant, a credit union, a hair salon, an alternative school, or a coffee shop, each participant must have the skill required to fulfill his or her assigned roles. Beyond knowing their individual parts, the group must have a clearly defined vision that anchors all activity, and they need to have a working knowledge of how the component parts come together to produce the product or service. They need to understand the product or service from their customers' perspective if they intend to stay in business.

2. If participants don't have the required skills, they must learn them in order to be productive and support the

process. Otherwise, they will certainly be instrumental in its demise.

3. Even if participants already have the required skill sets to perform their roles, they must be able to understand and act on communications that keep the team abreast of critical issues. They must understand and be committed to the "big picture" in order to be instrumental to its success. This is especially true for small, grassroots projects.

4. Harmony among an organization's participants is critical to success. Lack of understanding and/or commitment erodes trust. It erodes the capacity to believe in the mission. Participants withdraw input from their "best self." The project literally implodes from within.

If you are a participant in a success-networking project, we recommend that you insist on being trained before assuming a role in the project. We recommend that you insist that the project's vision, mission, and principles be included in the training. Otherwise, you might be the fall guy when, not if, the project fails.

Bottom line, before embarking on any major project that is dependent upon team participation, make sure that your team not only has the required technical skills to get the job done, but that yours is a learning organization capable of adapting to change and rising to whatever the project demands. Make sure that participants in your organization are open to learning; otherwise, their resistance to learning will become barriers to your success.

Barriers to learning

Barriers to learning are seldom addressed by project leaders, teachers and facilitators. Many behave as if they assume learning takes place simply because they walk into a classroom or boardroom and give a lecture on subject matter. In this scenario, information is imparted and sometimes supported through handouts or electronic matter. Corporations and educational institutions can check the "training received" box; technically, they have fulfilled their mission. In one sense, perhaps they did fulfill the mission, but did learning take place?

If learning did not take place, the desired knowledge level of behavior often falls short of expectations. When it's time for people to follow through on what was spoken, written, or taught in some other way, they can't perform at an acceptable level. If the intended outcome of the learning exercise did not happen, then the "training" or "notice" did not work. Your success-networking project is much too important to take this chance. Results are what counts. Effective learning is too important to its success.

Cause of Barriers

Experts agree that there are numerous obstacles to learning.

1. Learning new things means change. Change brings about fear of the unknown.

2. Adults often perceive that you are saying something is wrong with their performance when training is suggested. As a result, training is resisted.

3. People must believe that they will be positively impacted by whatever they must learn; otherwise, they believe that their time is wasted. No one likes for somebody else to waste their time.

4. If an individual has no previous positive learning experiences, they will not be enthusiastic about training. They will probably see it as another chance to fail.

5. It could be that some participants are not interested in the project. If this is the case, you'll have to rethink your participant choices.

Overcoming Barriers

Awareness of obstacles to learning is the first step in ensuring that information that is imparted is retained and understood by learning participants.

If you are the person charged with developing training materials for your project, make sure that your learners see its relevance. That way, it will be perceived as worth their time.

For instance, if you tell a group of people that they have to go through a self-analysis, many adults will immediately dismiss the course as useless -probably worse than useless. On the face of it, it sounds meddlesome.

On the other hand, if you explain precisely and clearly how they will immediately benefit from the course, you might have a different reaction. In this case, benefits might include discovering their greatest strengths so they can be used to support the project. A perceived benefit could also be the opportunity to do what they're already good at. A benefit that is transferable to just about any situation is an improved ability to communicate with just about anybody. If learning is made relevant (useful), imparted in a forum and format that permits practice and demonstrated success, and participants are permitted to learn from mistakes, learning barriers can be mitigated.

Let's continue with this example. When you take the learning process a step further, and have each learner write down their strengths and how they will use this knowledge to improve their life outside of the success-networking project, you will have demonstrated a great value-added component. You might also incorporate demonstrations that dramatically show how understanding communication preferences (such as Myers-Briggs profiles) immediately elevate a person's interaction skills.

Getting results should be incorporated into the entire training content. Reflections that capture learning milestones and how they can be incorporated in daily life help cement relevance. Presentations that incorporate understanding of subject matter by learners help bolster their confidence.

These kinds of activities, when incorporated into the teaching process, demonstrate that learning is more than a "project requirement." It demonstrates results that will radically improve the lives of learners far beyond the classroom experience.

A successful learning process follows specific laws that we call Laws of Learning. While the learning content will differ with each topic, the process remains the same. The Laws of

Learning are a guide for constructing learning content for any project.

Laws of Learning

The components of the Laws of Learning include: Information; Repetition; Role Model/Example; Pattern/Plan; Practice; and Mastery and Skill.

1. Information

All learning begins with information. What you need to know in order to perform a task, make a decision, or solve a problem are all bits of information.

In the preceding section, we talked about barriers to learning and how to overcome them. However, you, the learner, are ultimately responsible for your results. Your mindset about learning determines if this process is easy or difficult.

People who eagerly embrace new learning find digesting new information easier than those who are not yet convinced that an attitude of lifelong learning is critical in the 21st century. Global communications permit information to be shared and updated faster than we can assimilate it. If we are not open to listen, evaluate, and decide how to use relevant information, we are being left behind.

Your success in life, and as a success-networking participant, requires the following:

1. Willingness to accept new learning

2. Willingness to renew your mind
3. Willingness to admit weaknesses, including what you don't know

No matter what your status in life, you have to be willing to become the pupil.

Willingness to accept new learning

Learning begins with a desire for information - a desire to know. Without the desire, nothing will happen. In order to embrace the reality of concepts offered in this book, you must be prepared to learn.

Information is around us, seeking to break through the noise of daily living. How many times has the very answer you needed been at your fingertips, yet you didn't recognize it. You must first acknowledge that your preconceptions or beliefs may not be totally accurate. That simple act opens your mind to receive new information. Remaining "bull-headed" and "all-knowing" guarantees that new information will not penetrate your closed mind. On the other hand, once you deem the information critical, you will stop at nothing to seek it.

The first bit of information we suggest you seek to learn is information about you. Consider this: How do you know which information to look for if you don't know what's important to you? It follows that the most important information needed to plan the rest of your life is "Who are you? What is your passion, your vision, your lifelong dream – your very purpose in life?" Unless and until you can answer these questions, you may stumble around in a sea of information that has little relevance, resulting in little to no learning.

Knowing your purpose is a super motivator to learn. If your purpose is to show others how to turn rubbish into artwork but you are scared to death of speaking to a crowd, then you might be motivated to learn how to overcome your fear of speaking to groups. If your purpose is to share your knowledge of financial instruments on the credit union project, but you don't know how to write a definitive process outline, you might be motivated to learn how to do so.

What is your passion? What do you want to leave as a legacy for others? What do you need to learn in order to make your dream come alive? The time to start seeking and finding this information is now.

Don't wait for a formal class to begin assembling information about you. There are a number of tools that help you discover your strengths, passion, and purpose. The first doesn't cost a cent; you need only pay attention to your inner self. Since information is critical to pushing the re-set button on your life and embracing abundant living, it is highly recommended that you start now finding your purpose, your personal seat of power. Resources are listed in the "Resources" area at the back of this book.

Willingness to Renew Your Mind

Have you ever heard the statement "Black people can't work together?" We bring this up because we often hear this as an excuse for the failure of a project. Those who hold this belief might read books and other writings on Black towns, such as Boley and Tulsa, Oklahoma, and many other towns throughout the U.S. When you consider how these people worked together to make their vision a reality despite the incredible odds they faced, we believe that you will be convinced that Black people have worked together to achieve greatness, and continue to do so every day.

However, if your core belief system is that "Black people can't work together," you might consider renewing your mind before embarking on a project that includes Black people. You must first acknowledge that your preconceptions or beliefs may not be totally accurate.

Another core belief held by many is "there is only so much stuff that supports prosperity in the universe, and in order for me to get my share someone else is going to have to give up something." In this "zero sum game" scenario, collaborating with others on a success-networking project is going to be difficult at best. Serious mind-renewal will have to take place before you can be a fully supportive participant.

We are by no means suggesting that you and your team must be totally aligned in every belief. Diverse beliefs and points of view are arguably critical to creating the best possible solutions to a problem. Failure to consider differences, and the new ideas that emerge from them, causes stagnation and ultimately will kill a project or institution.

Renewal of the mind is more about the willingness to consider a perspective that is based upon new information.

Willingness to acknowledge weaknesses; lack of understanding

So often leaders and wannabe leaders will refuse to acknowledge that they don't personally have whatever it takes to get the job done. Here's the irony: people around you probably already know that you don't know. Few people live in a vacuum; they have other sources of information. Better that you admit you don't know - and seek to find out - than try to bluff your way through ignorance.

Once you have information and are willing to digest it, you're well on your way to obtaining knowledge that supports achieving success.

2. Repetition

Read it, say it, hear it, and teach it.

Learning occurs through many channels. It is best retained when layered through multiple channels. Reading, as in reading this book, is one channel. Reading it aloud increases your chance of remembering. Have you ever written a letter, then read it aloud and was astonished by the content? The ear has a way of clearing up foggy mental images.

Enhanced understanding often opens up as many questions as it answers, and therefore expands learning as new answers are found.

Learning is about obtaining, understanding, and applying new information. Practice makes perfect. Let's say you took our advice and learned more about your personal strengths, including your true passion in life. Put that learning to use. Begin to practice using your strengths and embracing your passion. You'll get better and better at it, becoming a recognized expert at it.

Becoming an expert adds great value to your life. It could change your life forever. Imagine the gift your expertise could bring to a project!

3. Role Model/Example

Learn from the past, from others who have already walked in your shoes. It speeds up the learning process by reducing the learning curve. It doesn't mean that you do exactly what they did, nor does it mean that they will do your work for you. Examine what they tell and show you. Do your homework about the process. Then apply critical thought to the process that your role model followed as you apply appropriate parts to your own project.

If you're interested in learning how to become an expert golfer, you will probably study the techniques of Tiger Woods or Jack Nicholas. If it's basketball, your choice might be Michael Jordan. Should your interest be teaching, John C. Maxwell or Marva Collins might become role models, depending on your focus. The point is, role models help us accelerate learning not only what works, but how it works as well.

We are all unique individuals, so one person's success story can rarely be unilaterally applied to another. However, you can apply someone else's successful process to your own unique set of circumstances.

Who are your role models? Who are the people who embody what you want to accomplish?

Request a meeting with them, either in person or via email. Fear of rejection might cause you to dismiss this as impossible. It is not! Contact them and tell them exactly what you want to accomplish, and why you want them to share some of their time with you. Don't expect to get a favorable response from all of them. Be diligent in your pursuit, and you will be surprised by many who are willing to give back by sharing information with you.

4. Pattern/Plan

A vision and a plan are critical to your achieving any goal you set.

What is the first thing that you hear when you're trying to start a business? Get a business plan! Failed businesses can often be attributed to failure to have and follow a clearly defined plan. The process can get bumpy even with a plan; without one, you don't have a prayer.

Nothing happens without an affirmative act on your part. Waiting "for your ship to come in" is just that – a lifelong wait with nothing to show for your time. If you sit and wait for the world to come to you, you will probably find yourself among the unfortunate majority who are told to sit down, line up, be quiet, and wait.

If your heart's desire is to be a great trumpet player, hopefully your parents started you in that direction with your first trumpet at an early age. If they didn't, your plans should include acquiring the instrument and gaining extensive experience on it. If you're serious about it, you'll study techniques used by some of the masters. You can take your pursuit to the next level by tapping into your personal network.

You can access suggested action plans on just about any topic by going to your local library and looking up references on your desired topic. You can start right now by "Googling" the topic on your computer.

As a commercial airline pilot, Dr. Higginbotham often cites having a flight plan as a perfect example of having a plan. Without it, he cannot be permitted to take to the skies and with good reason - he'd wander aimlessly and cause untold disaster!

5. Practice

How many times have you read about successful athletes who spend eight or more hours a day making sure that they are in topnotch shape in their craft? Imagine how many practice shots Michael Jordan took during his heyday. Great speakers didn't wake up one day at the top of their form. No one does. It takes practice.

As mentioned earlier, repetition builds learning. The more you do it, the more you learn about your craft.

Build a support network as you improve your skills. Encouragement is critical; it keeps the spirit positive. Faith in yourself and in a Higher Power can be critical to staying with your plan because the world can be cruel if you permit it. Stay strong, stay focused, stay in Faith, and you will persevere.

6. Mastery & Skill

Steven K. Scott, in his book *The Richest Man Who Ever Lived*, suggests that the key to winning every race is becoming diligent. Scott's definition of diligence is: "A learnable skill that combines creative persistence, a smart-working effort rightly planned and rightly performed in a timely, efficient, and effective manner to attain a result that is pure and of the highest quality of excellence."

According to Scott's writings, here are some of the rewards that come with diligence:

1. Advantage over others in the race

2. In control of the situation instead of being controlled by the situation

3. Experience true fulfillment

4. Respect and admiration

5. Needs satisfied

6. Ever increasing success

7. Efforts will be profitable

Diligence is required to attain mastery and skill.

The most obvious Mastery level performances are in the sports arena, primarily because achievements are widely publicized. We immediately think of people like Muhammad Ali, Michael Jordan, and Tiger Woods. In business we think about people like Steve Jobs, Warren Buffet, and Bill Gates, and of course there is Oprah Winfrey.

Notice that some of these people are not known for their principled behavior. But it is difficult to argue that they did achieve mastery and skill at what they do. They could not have done so without practicing the skill of diligence.

Section I Learning Activities

As mentioned earlier in this section, the first critical bit of information that you need comes from within. You have to learn what is important to you so you can use learning wisely. We are bombarded with so much information that we're in overload. How do you know which information to accept or seek if you don't know what's important to you?

Complete the form below to clarify what is important to you and what you want to accomplish in life. This will help you better focus on learning goals.

Passion What I love to do	Talent What I'm good at
Values What is important	Purpose What I was born to do

Based upon what I want to accomplish in life, I need to learn more about:

_____

_____

_____

_____

Possible mentors that can help me accomplish my goals are:

_____

_____

_____

_____

Make this commitment to action: "I have made arrangements to work with one or more of the mentors identified above."

SECTION II:
SUCCESS AND NETWORKING, DEFINED

While success-networking does not refer to success at networking, successful networks are critical in forming a success-networking system.

It is critical that those who wish to experience the success-networking system understand the importance of a success mindset. It is also necessary that you understand the importance of networks.

Success

What is Success? Is it a good thing or a bad thing?

Is it a journey or is it a destination? Is it power? Is it wealth? Is it a goal? Is it happiness? Is it a possession? What is this thing called success? What does it look like?

Let's look at what is said about success. In the Bible, the Lord God speaks to Joshua about success. Joshua 1:8 states "This book of the law shall not depart out of thy mouth; but thou shalt meditate therein day and night that thou may observe to do, according to all that is written therein: for then thou shall make thy *way* prosperous, and then thou shalt have **good** success."

The verse talks about the *law* (systematic-processes). The word *way* is used, which implies a *journey.* Note the word *good* - the opposite of good is bad. It implies that one could possibly experience bad success.

Success can be defined as the ***progressive realization of a predetermined worthwhile goal while enjoying the pursuit.*** This definition tells us that the discipline to prioritize and the ability to work toward a stated goal are essential to achieving success. It also suggests that the journey should be enjoyable.

Leadership development expert John Maxwell, in his book *Your Road Map to Success*, says, "Success is knowing your purpose in life, growing to reach your maximum potential and sowing seeds to benefit others."

Author Napoleon Hill in his book, *The Law of Success*, states, "Success in this world is always a matter of individual effort, yet you will only be deceiving yourself if you believe that you can succeed without the co-operation of other people. Success is a matter of individual effort to the extent that each person must decide in his or her own mind, what is wanted. This involves the use of the imagination. From this point on, achieving success is a matter of skillfully and tactfully inducing others to co-operate. Before you can secure co-operation from others; nay, before you have the right to ask for or expect co-operation from other people, you must first show a willingness to co-operate with them."

Success, simply stated, is a journey, knowing your purpose in life, learning continuously, and applying correct principles along the way. True success goes beyond material gain; it takes the total human experience into consideration.

How do *you* define success? Copy and complete the exercise at the end of this section. It will begin to inform you about your vision, principles, and destiny. Hopefully, this book will help you redefine success in a way that contributes to your peace of mind, living your dreams, and living abundantly.

Networking

A trip to your basic, conventional dictionary defines network as: "Any netlike combination of filaments, lines, veins, passages, or the like; 2. A system of interrelated buildings …; 3. RADIO-TV a group of transmitting stations linked by wire or microwave relax…"

It is interesting to note that there was no mention of people networks. The New World Dictionary has as its fifth selection: "a group, system, etc. of interconnected or cooperating individuals."

Despite what seems to be an absence of consideration for the term "networking" as it relates to the organization of people, we are witnessing, in people networking, the most dynamic component of the transition to a new information society. Networking is creating a dramatic impact socially, politically, and economically.

John Naisbitt, in his best-selling book *Megatrends*, identifies networking as one of the "ten new directions transforming our lives." In it he says, "Looking around at the world, it was clear to many that the problem of the day – a sagging economy, political unrest, and a litany of intractable social problems – were not solvable in a world organized according to the hierarchical principle. What was there to do? The answer to that question describes the way the new networking model evolved.

Networking was a powerful tool for social action. Those who would change the world began doing it logically in clusters of like-minded people with a single ideological purpose."

What is a "people" network? Simply stated, networks are people talking to each other, sharing ideas, information, and resources. Networks exist to foster self-help, to exchange information, to share resources, to improve productivity and work life, and to change society. Networks can be intimate and immediate – at times they serve as our extended families, bonding people together as strongly as bloodlines.

To understand networking is to discover its tremendous value and opportunity.

Why is it that you have not been involved in the networking process to its fullest potential? Perhaps it's because you have been programmed to believe that the best way to achieve success is to do it alone. Perhaps it is because you have not encountered a structure that convinced you of its efficacy and capabilities. A successful network, operating at its fullest synergistic potential, has a value far greater than the sum of its participants' individual efforts.

Unfortunately, our programming to "go it alone" has been so ingrained that we fail to believe even when the facts are clearly presented before our own eyes. Even when we engage in the networking process, we usually approach the process from a very individualistic perspective. Just hearing the term 'networking' evokes thoughts of utilizing others in a network for one's personal gain. Yet, networks and networking are used every day to find practical solutions to problems and answers to questions. For example, we turn to our network to find people we know that can help us acquire a better job, or sell a product, or even to acquire a mate. Complete the exercise at the end of this section to quickly determine your potential network partners.

Although we already utilize networks to a degree (church, social and political organizations, credit unions, etc.), we have not embraced the concept for mutual economic and real political gain. We have not explored networks from a position of personal values – trust, sharing, integrity, and faith. And we certainly haven't explored what it can eventually mean to our communities.

The questions that must be answered before beginning this journey are: "Are you ready for change? Are you willing to learn? Are you willing to explore a world larger than the one you've already been exposed to, including ideas that are new to you?"

In order to incorporate success networking into your life, you must be willing to learn. Without learning, we all continue to pay the price of ignorance.

Section II Learning Activities

In Section I Learning Activities, you identified what you want to accomplish in life, what you need to learn in order to accomplish your goals, and potential mentors who can help you.

In the space that follows, write a list of the **successes that you have experienced** in your life (using the traditional definition of success).

_____

_____

_____

_____

_____

_____

_____

_____

_____

The scope of your success could very well depend on your personal networks. Each of us should have a ready list of our existing support networks. Create your list in the table that follows.

Your Personal Network

These are people whom you know that may be able to help connect you to organizations that could benefit from your message. If your contacts don't have a direct connection to your potential audience, they may know someone else who has such a connection.

Name (include phone/email)/ Organization, Etc.	

Moments of Contemplation

Fools die for want of wisdom.
Proverbs 10:21

A brutish man knoweth not; neither doth a fool understand this.
Psalms 92:6

And the whole earth was of one language, and of one speech.
Genesis 11:1

SECTION III:
A BASIS FOR CHANGE

It has often been said that necessity is the mother of invention. In other words, when you are backed into a corner and your survival is threatened, you would be surprised at how creative you can become. In order to heighten your awareness of the need for change, let us explore the price of ignorance, the extent to which our society is out of balance, and whether or not our survival is threatened and at issue.

When we wrote the 1st edition of *Collaboration, Teamwork, and Networking* we stated that a state of emergency existed on economic and political fronts. That was 2004. As we prepare to go to press with the 2nd edition of our book, it is clear (and unfortunate) that the economic crash that we predicted has happened. Look at some of the major indicators.

Jobs and bank changes

In 2004, the highest number of annual FDIC (Federal Deposit Insurance Corporation) bank closings was 11 during 2002, according to the official FDIC website. Since that time, particularly during the past 2 years, the number of closings has increased more than tenfold.

Bank Closing: 2005 – 2010

Year	Number of Closings
2005	0
2006	0
2007	1
2008	25
2009	140
2010	167

Banks go under when they are no longer able to meet their obligations. They might be unable to pay the bills, or a bank failure may arise because they can't provide cash when depositors demand it. Although FDIC banks offer insurance protection to its clients within a pre-defined ceiling amount, their closings are indications of economic problems in the marketplace.

In 2006, the national unemployment rate was 5%, according to the Bureau of Labor Statistics. In December 2010, it was 9.4%. That translates to 14.5 million people. The unemployment rate for Blacks is 15.8% - much higher than the national average.

What does this mean? As if our readers don't already know, it means that many people in our communities are out of a job, with no immediate prospects in sight. It means that the problems are much broader than our own communities. It is beyond nationwide. It is worldwide.

The price of ignorance

Do you remember the phrase, "What you don't know won't hurt you?" A childish phrase at best. Where did it originate? Is it part of the programming? Unfortunately, many such phrases carried throughout one's life could not have been more wrong.

The price of not knowing, i.e., the price of ignorance, has been and continues to be the most painful and burdensome payment of human existence. If information is power, then the lack of information is impotence. Whole nations have been and continue to be enslaved as a price paid for ignorance. Maybe you can't relate to the enslavement of distant nations. So let's bring it closer to home. What price are you paying?

Freedom vs. Slavery

"Ignorance deprives men of freedom because they do not know what alternatives there are. It is impossible to choose to do what one has never heard of." – **Ralph Barton Perry**

Are you locked in a rat race that deprives you of the freedom to make appropriate choices for you and your family? Consider your job, your skills, your income level, your neighborhood, and your influence. According to the dictionary, **freedom** is the "exemption or liberation from the control of some arbitrary power," and **slavery** is "a condition of submission to or domination by some influence." It is understandable that there would be a heavy denial at the notion that slavery is still alive and well in this "free society." So, let's explore this notion a little deeper.

In the exercise that immediately follows, answer "yes" or "no" as to whether or not the following life conditions are those of slavery; and second, answer "yes" or "no" as to whether or not those conditions are present in our society.

SLAVERY	LIFE CONDITIONS	PRESENT
_____	DEPENDENCY	_____
_____	CONTROLLED	_____
_____	NO AUTHORITY	_____
_____	LOW WAGES	_____
_____	JOB DISSATISFACTION	_____
_____	INSECURITY	_____
_____	IGNORANCE	_____
_____	DISEASE	_____
_____	HELPLESSNESS	_____
_____	APATHY	_____
_____	SPIRITUAL	_____

Slavery is a condition of an economic system.

Education is a fundamental factor in economics, as no country can achieve sustainable economic development without substantial investment in human capital. What do you know about economics? Do you participate in or even influence those decisions that are being made on a daily basis that have an effect on your life – socially, politically, and economically? If you don't understand economics and you depend on others to make the right decisions on your behalf, you will never be free.

Consider that ignorance can mean the difference between wealth and poverty, brotherhood and racism, and life and death. What higher price can be paid for *not knowing*? Consider that information is proliferating at an overwhelming rate and that the total of human knowledge is doubling almost annually. It should become apparent that the probability of falling deeper into the abyss of ignorance has increased. It should also become apparent that you have been unable to access even the most essential information without enlisting the help of others. Through default, you already participate in informal networking each day of your life. Can there be a stronger endorsement for effective, systematic, and focused networking?

A society out of balance

Perhaps the most pressing justification for change is the fact that our society, the post-industrialized society, is irreversibly out of balance socially, politically, and economically. Like a mortally damaged ship, it is slowly sinking, leaving us with one of two choices - abandon the ship or go down with it. The laws of nature have proven that a body out of balance too long will perish.

We have the highest rate of illiteracy and disease in our history. Deceit, greed, and crime have permeated all levels of our society. For instance, according to a 2005 study by Michael I. Norton of Harvard Business School and Dan Ariely of Duke University, in the United States the top wealth quintile (1/5th of the population) owns 84% of the total wealth, the 2nd quintile owns about 10%, and the third wealth quintile about 5%. The 4th and 5th wealth quintile own .2% and .1%, respectively, of the total U.S. wealth. When the top tier of the wealthy, such as Donald Trump, talks about such mind-blowing trinkets of consumption as luxury residences in Connecticut, Manhattan, and Palm Beach; a Boeing 727; a 282-foot yacht; and a black jet helicopter he picked up for $8 million, it amplifies the imbalance of wealth, and the gap continues to widen.

When our entertainers can live in a 41,000 square feet mansion on 5 acres in Bel Air, California while at the same time urban dwellers get by in new projects where 600 square feet is spacious and millions are homeless, our society is out of balance.

The Center for Arms Control and Non-proliferation, a Washington, D.C.-based 501(c)3 non-profit, non-partisan research organization dedicated to enhancing international peace and security in the 21st century, posted an interesting report as of March 11, 2010. They indicated that the Pentagon's budget increased dramatically since 2001. In inflation-adjusted dollars, the total defense budget grew from $432 billion in FY01 to $720 billion in FY11, a real increase of approximately 67 percent. The Pentagon's base budget, which excludes war and nuclear weapons funding, grew steadily over the last decade, increasing from $390 billion in FY01 to $540 billion in FY11, a real increase of 38 percent. These are statistics that we should all know. We should think about what they mean to our safety and to our economy. We should think about what this spending trend means to our children and grandchildren. When you participate in the system by at least keeping abreast of what is going on, you are in a position to impact decisions rather than have them roll over you.

A society that truly prospers is a society in balance. It recognizes the balance *between* the social, political, and economic systems and a balance *within* those systems. The overriding principle of our society is "Economic Determinism." Economic determinism is defined as "the doctrine that all social, cultural, political, and intellectual forms are determined by or results from economic factors such as the quality of natural resources, productive capability, technological development, or the distribution of wealth." The consequence of this doctrine has precipitated such a focus on the creation of wealth at all costs that our institutions of religion, health, education, finance, business, and government are falling apart. The equation for that process is ***DECEIT + GREED = CONTROL = WEALTH.***

Have you heard the expression, "What goes around comes around," or perhaps, "Whatsoever ye soweth, so shall you reap?" Well, one of the physical laws of nature is that energy is constant. Whatever energy you put out into the energy fields stays there, and could eventually return to you.

Our society will not correct itself by waiting for the few at the top to change their behavior patterns. It will not correct itself with the rhetoric of political pundits or from the efforts of our most charismatic political leaders. It won't come from the heads of big business or the advent of some technological breakthrough. The downward spiral will only correct itself when the everyday people come together in organized, knowledgeable, and economically able teams, committed to the enhancement of humankind and the planet.

Political suicide (Become Involved!)

Let's explore the definition of suicide.

Suicide: 1. The intentional taking of one's own life; 2. Destruction of one's own interest or prospects.

Whether through ignorance or by neglect, with regards to the political process, our lives are being taken away and our interests or prospects are being destroyed. The real test is whether or not we can acknowledge, accept and *take responsibility* for our ignorance and/or our neglect. If we can't, the track upon which we're traveling will lead us into an abyss – nowhere and nothing. The devastation of "political suicide" will continue to reign.

Question! How many new bills were passed into law in your state during the past two years? Do you know? Let's make it real easy for you. Can you name three of the new laws? Seems to me we have a real problem here if you can't. More importantly, we may have discovered a source/cause of many of our community problems.

For your information, the number of new laws passed in your state each year is staggering. In Missouri alone, the House of Representatives 96th General Assembly has 624 bills and resolutions on its docket. These are in addition to the local and federal laws. And most of us can't name three of these new laws. Whom do the laws affect? You're right - they affect *us.* And guess what? Since we did not participate in their drafting or passing, there is a very strong probability that our best interests may not have been served.

Consider that this year there will be laws passed regarding how much income you can earn and keep; laws regarding the size, type, and location of shelter you can own; laws regarding the air you breathe, the food you eat, and the water you drink; and, the information you can receive and/or deliver. These laws are at the very core of your survival as well as the survival of your neighbors, friends, associates, and family. If you don't care about yourself, care about your family, your children, and their children.

Many, but not all of us, participate in the political system by exercising the right to vote. If you do, how much does your vote count? Or perhaps a better question is: To what extent does your individual vote determine the outcome of these critical laws that so directly affect you?

Laws don't just happen. They don't get passed in a vacuum. Disinterested persons don't sponsor them. If you simply consider the costs in time, money, and human energy required to sponsor and introduce a new bill to the legislature, and to follow that bill through its passage into law, you would have to assume that someone, or some entity, or some consortium has a vested economic interest. After all, how much money would you spend on something that clearly would not benefit you? Or, put another way, how much money would you spend to protect the millions of dollars in revenue that you are receiving each year? Get the picture? The assumption naturally follows that your "non-vested" interests are not really being considered since it isn't you who put up the money. Who has the vested interest in laws regarding health care? Who has the vested economic interest in matters regarding military spending? The answers to these questions will identify the primary financial sources for the passage of our most important laws.

By now you are probably experiencing an idea shift, and, yes, you are perfectly right! It is your patriotic duty and a benefit of your citizenship to cast your vote. However, it is political suicide to cast that vote in ignorance or cast it without assurances that *your* best interests will be served. We must learn to become informed voting blocs because we have a political crisis.

How much does one vote count? One vote, standing alone, is like casting your fate to the wind. One vote, joined with others who are knowledgeable and who have an established economic base, makes a significant difference. Your one vote *then* becomes the key to your empowerment.

Health catastrophe

How can you refute the fact that we have a health catastrophe? The facts are truly frightening. According to the Center for Disease Control, in 2007, nearly 2.5 million people died in the United States, and half of those deaths were caused by heart disease and cancer. That's about 3,500 deaths each day. In one year, we lose more Americans from heart disease and cancer than from all of our wars combined. The cancer.org website reports that it expected over 1.5 million new cancer cases during 2010. And yet, no one acknowledges that *we have an epidemic.*

The air we breathe, the water we drink, and the foods we eat are killing us. Scientists report that a multitude of pollutants bombard the body daily, impairing the integrity of the immune system and compromising its ability to defend us. This not only shortens our lives, but erodes the quality of our years.

In every phase of production, our food is contaminated. There are pollutants in the soil from chemical fertilizers and pesticides, contaminated water for irrigation, hormones in animal feed, food additives, plastic packaging, and lead cans. To make matters worse, pesticides banned in the U.S. are sold to other countries and foodstuffs contaminated with them are imported back to us. As an example, about one third of U.S. fresh tomato consumption is imported, with the bulk coming from Mexico, according to the Agricultural Marketing Research Center. They are picked in a semi-ripe state and injected with gas to preserve them until they reach your table. We have to assume some responsibility for this process. After all, we demand "fresh" tomatoes year-round even though our local growth seasons cannot support them.

Toxic metal contamination, a source of food pollution, leads to fearsome diseases and to a host of degenerative disorders. Toxic metals commonly consumed are lead, aluminum, and mercury. Dangerous lead levels that can seriously affect our health are being found on many fronts. For example, in January 2011, USA Today reported that dangerous levels of lead were found in reusable bags distributed by popular grocery and drug store chains. The December 2010 issue of The Journal of Environmental Health reported that many items available for purchase throughout the United States — such as toys, home décor items, salvage, kitchen utensils and jewelry — contain surface lead concentrations more than 700 times higher than the federal limit. Concern over the impact of lead water service lines leading to homes prompted a January 2010 update from the National Center for Environmental Health on lead-based water lines. The FDA is no longer sure that *any* level of lead is safe. Switching to aluminum is no improvement. Aluminum is almost as poisonous as lead and harder for the body to get rid of. And, there are over a hundred sources of mercury pollution in the U.S.

Of all the environmental pollutants, radiation definitely has the quickest and most damaging effect. The levels of background radiation in our environment due to nuclear power plant accidents and nuclear weapons testing, as well as ozone layer depletion, x-rays, TVs, computer screens, microwave ovens, etc. have increased dramatically.

In case you haven't noticed, every pollutant, every contaminant, every toxic metal, and every rad of radiation of which we speak have a human partner in crime who extracted a substantial economic benefit. Forget about eating your Wheaties! We're about winning the game of life and we've chosen the community as our court.

Economic crash

When we wrote the 1st edition of *Teamwork, Collaboration, and Networking*, we posed the question: "Are we headed for an economic collapse?" At the time ominous signs were everywhere. New Wall Street scandals were surfacing daily; record highs and precipitous drops buffeted the Dow; Brazil, Mexico, and other emerging countries owed hundreds of billions of dollars that threatened many of the largest U.S. banks; farm debt totaled over $200 billion; and the entire U.S. savings and loan system was bankrupt. The gap between the rich and poor was wider than at any time since 1929. As recent as January 2009, the Centre for Research on Globalization wrote an article calling the U.S. the world's largest debtor.

During the past decade as our economy was beginning to unravel, politicians blindly insisted that we had a sound, prosperous economy. That was a fantasy akin to that of children who think that if they shut their eyes real tight, adults won't be able to see them. Recent experience proved that the U.S. economy could not withstand the level of damage done to it over several decades. We've suffered the economic losses – and the ethical bankruptcy – that results from Corporate America downsizing its employees, ruining farmers, squeezing out small businesses, stifling minority enterprise, reducing people's paychecks, and shutting the escape hatch for the poor. From manufacturing to oil production, from agriculture to home building, whole industries are deep in the dumps.

The globalization of the world, including its nations' economies, has made our economic situation more complicated that it was in earlier years. The economic situation that we face in the U.S. is tied to what is occurring around the globe. For instance, global wheat prices more than doubled in the second half of 2010, according to a report from the World Bank. We are already experiencing huge price increases at the grocery stores. We are experiencing difficulty maintaining a roof over our heads. This is a substantially more serious problem than having difficulty filling our gas tanks or heating our homes. Based upon the degree of hardship faced by a large sector of our population, it's safe to say that our economic system is in peril. It's not marked by some stock market event like the crash of 1929, and it is not a single, major impending event. It is a global, present-day, ongoing happening.

Let's take a walk down memory lane. We can learn a lot from our past. It's been said, "A lesson not learned will soon be repeated." Take a look at what was reported in the May 1988 edition of *Mother Jones Magazine*...

1. *Since 1981, more than 620,000 productive farm families were put out of business.*

2. *The rate of small business failures jumped dramatically in the '80s, with 56,000 going under in 1986 alone.*

3. *From the end of World War II until 1981 (36 years), only 170 banks failed in the United States. In the 7 years from 1981 to 1988, 621 banks failed, with the number increasing sharply each year.*

4. *An estimated 12 million Americans lost their jobs since 1981 as a result of plant closings and layoffs. For those laid off, there is only a 62% chance of finding another job within a year.*

5. *More than 44% of the new jobs created in our economy during the '80s pay less than $7,400 a year — 35% less than a poverty level income for a family of four.*

6. *The number of Americans having to work in jobs paying the $3.35 an hour minimum wage ($6,968 a year) grew from 5.1 million in 1981 to 7.8 million in 1987.*

7. *Since 1979 there was a 35% increase in the number of families with children living in poverty.*

It's over 20 years later and, although many changes for the better have occurred, many of the same conditions persist. We've been courting a Depression because, among other issues, our nation's production economic base is still crumbling.

The questions remain: Is there a basis for change? Can we continue along the same road that we've tried before? Does this road lead to failure and self-destruction? Even the wealthiest among U.S. citizens must by now admit that our systems are crumbling and it's time for a change. Although we can't expect the wealthy to initiate change on behalf of the not-so-wealthy, change is inevitable. Like the line from a song, "everything must change, nothing remains the same." And, from the burning embers of a decaying industrial society, a New Society has emerged.

What are you doing about it?

Can you make a difference?

Perhaps at this point in your reading you have acknowledged a time for change, and you may have acknowledged a requirement to link with others in order to manifest a change. However, we have only scratched the surface of the programmed baggage that you still carry. Therefore, we must continue to build our case. "The New Society" further legitimizes the team concept while preparing the soil of optimism for our crossing over.

The issue of survival

There is an old but true adage: "The hardest thing to open is a closed mind." One of the most frustrating experiences is trying to help an ailing loved one who, operating on false data, is unwilling to accept good information that would help them survive because they refuse to believe the messenger – you. Have you had a similar experience? We must learn to listen, and be less anxious to shoot the messenger because the message disturbs our comfort zone by making us face the truth.

Unfortunately, our survival – yours and mine – is at issue, and the issue has reached a crisis point. We are in the midst of political turmoil – at home and abroad. Catastrophic health issues now affect our children, with childhood obesity now causing diseases heretofore unheard of in young children. It is also safe to say that we are experiencing a global economic crisis. In the face of overwhelming evidence of such catastrophic consequences, the mass reaction appears to be apathy or worse, denial.

The more learned or "intelligent" segment of the general population addresses the issues in academic discussion, but fail to act.

The middle segment of the general population perceives the issues as irrelevant, or at least resting comfortably in the hands of those who can best decide. They seem to have a reverence for technology and American invincibility. They block out the possibility of unpleasant consequences and do nothing. They continue to say, "If we can put a man on the moon, surely we can cure cancer." This group is reluctant to look behind the curtain at forces that might be maintaining policies that are hurtful to them.

The segment of the general population that is at the lower end of the economic spectrum appears to be numb to the existence of the issues, so of course they do nothing. This segment is kept busy in day-to-day survival. Their concerns are: "Where am I going to lay my head, and where is my next meal coming from? If I can't make it through tomorrow, who cares about national and global issues?"

The irony is that the masses are the only ones who can bring about a change. Those "leaders" on whom we have depended have helped foster the problem. If we are to survive these catastrophic consequences, and we believe we will, the masses can no longer afford to stand on the sidelines. We must come together, become more aware of the issues, take our positions, and commence taking charge through strategic, proactive behavior.

Only you can decide if you will become an agent of change, or continue to support the status quo. Understand that there is a price to pay, whatever your choice.

It is our hope that you will elect the door that says the price of ignorance is too high, open the doors of your mind, and take an active stance against impending political suicide, health catastrophes, and an economic disaster.

Section III Learning Activities

A Basis for Change begs a question that each of us needs to ask ourselves. That question is: "Do we believe there is a need for change in our personal life and/or in our community?"

We urge our readers to consider the question after reading Section III. If your answer is "yes," please write on a separate piece of paper what you consider to be a **basis for change**, and **the price we will pay** if there is not change within ourselves or our community.

This link provides additional resources that offer insight into the issues that face African-Americans in the U.S.: http://www.llife.org/insights.htm.

Topics at this link include *12 Things The Negro Must Do For Himself* by Nannie Helen Burroughs; *Plight Deepens for Black Men, Studies Warn* by Erik Eckholm; *They are Still Our Slaves*, an article Dee Lee read on a New York radio station; *The Black Matrix* (revised 2009) by Franklin G. Jones; and *21 Things African-Americans Need to Do, according to Tavis Smiley*.

SECTION IV:
THE NEW SOCIETY

Alvin Toffler opens his 1980 best-seller, *The Third Wave*, with the lines: "A new civilization is emerging in our lives, and blind men everywhere are trying to suppress it… Pieces of this new civilization exist today. Millions are already attuning their lives to the rhythms of tomorrow. Others, terrified of the future, are engaged in a desperate, futile flight into the past and are trying to restore the dying world that gave them birth. The dawn of this new civilization is the single most explosive fact of our lifetime. Humanity faces a quantum leap forward. It faces the deepest social upheaval and creative restructuring of all time. Without clearly recognizing it, we are engaged in building a remarkable new civilization from the ground up. This is the meaning of the Third Wave… With some intelligent help from us, this could turn out to be the first truly humane civilization in recorded history."

John Naisbitt, the author of the best-seller *Megatrends*, suggests: "We are living in the time of the parenthesis, the time between eras. Those who are willing to handle the ambiguity of this in-between period and to anticipate the new era will be a quantum leap ahead of those who hold on to the past. Although the time between eras is uncertain, it is a great and yeasty time, filled with opportunity. In the time of the parenthesis, we have extraordinary leverage – individually, professionally and institutionally – especially when endowed with a clear sense, a clear conception, a clear vision of the road ahead. Many people passionately resist the notion of an economy built on information and despite a wealth of evidence, deny the industrial era is over. We have to release this death-grip on the past and deal with the future."

Dr. Donald Cowan, a founding Fellow of the Dallas Institute of Humanities and Culture, and President Emeritus of the University of Dallas, said in a 1987 address: "We are now between two ages, on the threshold of a new epoch in human history. An age with which we are familiar has already ended; new forms and structures are carrying the burden of the energies of our society. Yet, educational systems in our time have largely ignored the realities of such a change and seek to restore the structures of a former epoch. Reluctant to enter a new age, we are at risk of mindlessly insisting on preserving the patterns of the old."

"A great burden will fall upon young people now of high school and college age. They will have to forge new economic and political structures to enhance rather than diminish individual freedoms. Theirs will be the responsibility for allowing new institutions to develop and old ones to decay when the constancy of overall wealth brings inevitable conflicts. The shifting of the basis of power will make civil strife exceedingly likely in the near future. But if wisdom in leadership is available, the nation can make the transition without violence."

"Nothing short of a complete rethinking of our entire educational scheme will suffice. It is evident that the beginning point for any solution to these problems lies in an education for all which emphasizes the full stature of the human person. A different mode of thinking will be required – one based on those imaginative forms that provide a vision of human nature and destiny, an invisible web of meaning within which learning takes on significance. And it is precisely this imaginative structure that educational systems have deliberately excluded."

It is important that you acknowledge the presence of this new society called the Information Age. We have already shifted into the new society. The old society, the Industrial Age, is decaying and going the way of the dinosaur. You are again at the crossroads and the signs say Industrial Society to the left and Information Age Society to the right. There is only one decision, and that is whether you want to hitch your wagon to a rising star or a falling star.

The new society brings its own set of social, political, and economic systems. And, if you are to prosper, you must learn the rules of the game.

Some of the characteristics of this new society, the Information Age, are:

1. Information-based vs. Industrial-based
2. People Power vs. Money Power
3. Global Economy vs. Domestic Economy
4. Participative Government vs. Representative Government

Information-based vs. Industrial-based

The takeaway here is that advancements in technology have enabled many jobs formerly held by people to be automated. The kinds of manufacturing jobs that propelled many into the middle class no longer exist. The Industrial Age economy has been replaced by one that has information as strategic resource. Most of the jobs that have been created during the past several decades have been in information, knowledge, or service areas. We are now a nation of information workers. With the coming of the Information Society, we have, for the first time, an economy based on a key resource that is not only renewable but self-generating.

Corporations are still grappling with management models that have not been retro-fitted to accommodate the rapid changes driven by global markets. As importantly, people have not shifted thinking in a way that permits readily adapting to the new reality. Why do you think that hiring managers are seeking younger people to fill new job openings? One of the attributes that this younger generation brings to the table is their comfort level with technology.

With information as the strategic resource, access to the economic system is much easier, aided by access to personal computers. You are in an excellent position to use this readily accessible information in a way that creates wealth.

People Power vs. Money Power

In the Industrial Age, power was generated by money. Remember the golden rule: "He who has the gold makes the rule?" In the Information Age, people who have organized to create wealth and influence the rules of governance will generate power. The catalyst for this shifting of power is the availability of information at all levels in the society.

Power is vested to those who control the means of production. In the Industrial Age, the sale of tangible products produced wealth. The means of producing those products was the factory, and the plant and equipment became the primary capital. This placed the wealth and power into the hands of the few who owned the factories and who, therefore, controlled the flow of essential information and knowledge.

In the Information Age, the sale of ideas and information produce the wealth. The means of producing an intangible product can be anywhere and at any time.

As a result, knowledge has become the primary capital in this new economic system because it has become more valuable than plant and equipment.

Additionally, information is proliferating at an overwhelming rate and man's knowledge is doubling almost annually. It can no longer be held by the few.

Armed with this new availability of knowledge and information, people are organizing under a variety of banners and are experiencing a new empowerment as they begin to change those conditions that don't align with their beliefs and principles.

Global Economy vs. Domestic Economy

With the transition to an Information Society, we move to a global economic system. If you mail a letter, it takes two to four days to arrive at its destination. If you send a letter electronically, it will take a couple of seconds. The person can elect to respond to your electronic letter within seconds, and you will have negotiated your business in less than hour rather than a week, accelerating life and commerce. Now, with the use of electronics to send money around the world at the speed of light, we have almost completely collapsed the money information float. With the shifting of industry to emerging nations and by being caught up in the rhetoric and dreams of the past, the United States has fallen from being the most prosperous nation on earth to the 10th (2010 Legatum Prosperity Index).

Participative Government vs. Representative Government

As more information is available and accessible, as more people are empowered, and the more centralized governments fail to address the issues of the constituents, more and more people will organize to change those system inequities. There has been a gradual, but pronounced, shift of power out of the hands of elected officials to direct ballot voting through local initiatives and referenda where people, not officials, decide by a majority vote a certain course of action. The guiding principle of this participatory democracy is that people must become more knowledgeable and must be a part of the process of arriving at decisions that affect their lives.

What does all this New Society really mean? It simply reinforces the reality that change is inevitable and that history is cyclical. The social, political, and economic systems that we have grown to understand and to recognize don't fit the reality of the current world environment. And when something doesn't fit, it is either changed or discarded. Consequently, we are at a time in history when our industrialized society is shedding its old skin and taking on a new one. This new skin, if you will, is still being formed and there is a tremendous opportunity to participate in its shaping. As John Naisbitt said: "Those who are willing to handle the ambiguity of this in-between period and to anticipate the new era will be a quantum leap ahead of those who hold on to the past." It is the best opportunity for grassroots Americans because we have little or no vested interest in the way things are. We have every reason, in addition to survival, for wanting things changed.

There is a natural and understandable reluctance toward activism. One consideration must be competing interests between existing responsibilities, with little time left over. Given day-to-day pressing needs and the temptation to travel the path of instant gratification, there is great temptation to say: "Live for today, the future will take care of itself." And, it is true that the future will take care of itself, but what kind of future will it be? *Will it be a future that you want for the next generation?*

Still not sure about this New Society talk? Maybe we can make it easier by going back in time to a similar period in history. You see, history *does* repeat itself. Your hesitance is something shared by all levels of the social, political, and economic scale. There is no need to feel awkward or alone in your reluctance to embrace the new reality. Rather, time would be better spent trying to understand its implications, then acting on your understanding.

There was a time in history, not so long ago as history counts, that the existing societal structure was struggling to hold on to the past while a new societal structure was trying to emerge. Things then were just the same as they are today, i.e., calamity and chaos reigned. Read the following letter from a very learned and distinguished gentleman and be your own judge about this old society/new society business. Perhaps then your views on "success-networking" will change. Perhaps you'll agree that it is a sensible vehicle for bridging the serious divides we face.

To: President Andrew Jackson

> *The canal system of this country is being threatened by the spread of a new form of transportation known as 'railroad.' The Federal government must preserve the canals for the following reasons:*
>
> *One. If canal boats are supplanted by 'railroads', serious unemployment will result. Captains, cooks, drivers, hostlers, repairman, and lock tenders will be left without means of livelihood, not to mention the numerous farmers now employed in growing hay horses.*
>
> *Two. Boat builders would suffer and tow-line, whip and harness makers would be left destitute.*

Three. Canal boats are absolutely essential to the defense of the United States. In the event of the expected trouble with England, the Erie Canal would be the only means by which we could ever move the supplies so vital to waging modern war.

For the above-mentioned reasons, the government should create an Interstate Commerce Commission to protect the American people from the evils of 'railroads' and to preserve the canals for posterity.

As you may well know, Mr. President, 'railroad' carriages are pulled at the enormous speed of 15 miles per hour by 'engines' which, in addition to endangering life and limb of passengers, roar and snort their way through the countryside, setting fire to crops, scaring the livestock, and frightening women and children. The Almighty certainly never intended that people should travel at such breakneck speed.

Martin Van Buren, Governor – New York January 31, 1829

It goes without saying that things changed, and now it's time to change again. Hopefully, you are beginning to see that our working together – in a formal, systematic structure – is the only tangible and logical vehicle for getting across a growing chasm. It is the only reasonable means to achieve successful living.

We call this vehicle Success-networking™. Turn the page to learn more about its foundation, structure, and how you, too, can make it work for you.

SECTION V:
SUCCESS-NETWORKING

How to Set Up and Run a Success-network System

The Success-networking™ Foundation: A Historical Perspective

Throughout the history of man and civilization, it has been repeatedly demonstrated that when people connect with other people, linking ideas and resources for a civil and moral cause to enhance the survival of humankind, the results have been dramatic and the process has been powerful.

Perhaps you can recall a young gentleman who got together with twelve (12) of his friends over 2,000 years ago and started a network. The cause was rooted in moral conviction, and their intention was to enhance the survival of humankind. They had a dinner and celebrated the cause of their network. Today, their network is still flourishing, although the cause has been somewhat tarnished and abused. The gentleman's name is Jesus Christ, his friends were called disciples. Their dinner was the Last Supper, and their network is named Christianity. Would you say that their network was powerful? Most would agree that power couldn't even begin to describe the essence and the impact of their network.

Eons later, there were two other young gentlemen who formed networks that you may recall. They, too, operated from a moral conviction, and their intention was to enhance the survival of humankind. One can draw parallels in the character of all three, and even in their deaths. The latter two young gentlemen were Mahatma Gandhi and Martin Luther King, Jr. They, too, formed incredibly powerful networks that changed the course of history.

Networking is powerful. And the highest order of power in networking occurs when the cause operates out of moral conviction (it is the right thing to do) and when the intention is to enhance humankind. It has the greatest and most lasting impact when the network incorporates the knowledge and utilization of economic systems.

What is very apparent about the evolutionary change discussed in this book is the effect of the quantum leap. The changes from the old society to the new society are not linear; they are multi-dimensional, and they are establishing a new paradigm. The new society is a dramatic change from the order and structure of our present societal systems, our organizations, our values, our lifestyles, our work patterns, our methods of thinking, our methods of communicating, etc. And, perhaps the most significant change of all (we'll be able to tell when we have had an opportunity to look back from the years ahead), is the change from an organizational structure that has been in place for thousands of years and has transcended all previous societal shifts, e.g., the shift from the agricultural society to the industrial society. The organizational structure in question is the hierarchical structure; the pyramid-shaped organizational structure that has served to empower the few and to denigrate the masses.

In the new society that we envision, building is from the bottom up. Solutions that provide desired change emerge from within the affected groups, rather than top-down. Thought leaders of the 21st century suggest that organizations encourage open and ongoing dialogue between and among people who actually perform work. It has become clear that this kind of exchange generates the best ideas. This also holds true for success networking. There are no rigid, hierarchical structures to slow down the information flow – just when speed and more flexibility are critically needed. The centralized institutions whose very existence relies upon hierarchies are crumbling everywhere, primarily through failure to operate from a moral high ground. Their failure to address issues that are front and center in the lives of the people they serve is causing their undoing. The advent of 21st century communication tools is enabling smaller, decentralized units to form. Witness the impact of Facebook, Twitter, and other networks where word travels at the speed of light. With the click of a mouse we can engage others in our own issues.

And so, when we identify success-networking at its highest order, we should add to the criteria that the model should not be hierarchical in organizational structure. It should be fluid and flexible; each individual is equal in importance; it should occur in small, autonomous units and not assume a large, organizational structure; and communication and decision-making should flow from the bottom to the top, from top to the bottom, and from side to side. This structural criterion is consistent with what we observe to be components of the Information Age economic system, i.e., people empowerment, shared wealth, decentralized, and politically participative. We are seeing today that the networks formed by both Gandhi and King are struggling for identity; that Christianity, although showing no evidence of demise, is having a strong identity crisis with respect to religion vs. spirituality. More importantly for this discussion, their problems stem from their hierarchical structures and all the ramifications of those structures.

As we continue to establish a pattern for the design of success-networking, we must consider longevity. An observation made by Lipnack and Stamp in their book entitled *Networking*, was that the networks rarely had longevity. This was attributed to the fact that they were usually formed for a specific purpose and when that purpose was achieved (or not achieved), they had considerable difficulty either holding together or trying to identify a new purpose for their existence.

Effective organizations can be focused on several initiatives concurrently if organized differently. For example, MADD (Mothers Against Drunk Driving) demonstrates the success of networking because of its effectiveness in legislative actions and growth rate success. Although we are 100% behind their cause, an argument can be made that they are tremendously underutilized as a success network simply because of their singular focus. Certainly, there are social, political, and economic issues and mutual membership concerns that could be addressed internally or through interlinking with other networking organizations. As an example, isn't the affliction of cancer and drug addiction as inhumane as alcohol? MADD could expand their success networking effectiveness if it decided to make a statement of support for organizations that battle these afflictions.

Let's reflect for a moment and review the historical foundation we've observed to be essential to *Success-networking*™.

1. Organize with moral conviction and a cause to enhance humanity

2. Knowledge and utilization of economic systems

3. Organize in a non-hierarchical structure

4. Ensure longevity through multi-dimensional goals

At its very core, our Success-networking™ model provides a solid foundation from which to build viable businesses with a built-in customer base ready to buy their products and services. It is the ultimate in prosumerism; people who produce goods and services and use the goods and services they produce. This process provides jobs within the community, builds wealth, circulates dollars within the community, and provides a tax base that supports improved services within the community.

Our view is that tens of thousands of organizations throughout the U.S. and beyond are poised to add economics driven success-networks to their existing activities. Churches and social organizations already possess much of what is required for success, including a need for change. The list below is by no means complete; it is aimed at showing you that you can start changing your personal lives, as well as lives of people within your community, beginning today.

Here's some of what you possess:

1. An adequate membership base (your immediate customers)
2. At least one strong unifying principle (you agree on important values)
3. An element of trust already exists among members

Below are needs that face most of our communities in urban areas:

1. Development of independent businesses amongst members is lacking; interdependence would be advantageous
2. There is a need for a stronger tax base within our communities
3. There is a need for a stronger voice within the political spectrum (put another way, when you try to change things individually, you don't have success)

The following are some businesses that, in most urban areas, will immediately bring value to your membership:

1. Credit Union (increase access to credit, funding for the needs of the organization)
2. Mortgage company (why depend on banks that don't provide the services your community needs)
3. Services, from Dry Cleaners to Beauty Supply Stores and everything in between (why spend dollars that don't support services within your own community)

You don't have to subscribe to the LLIFE Success-networking™ model that we use. Find one that you're comfortable with, and get started. You can also use this book as an aid to get started. However you start, action is better than inaction.

One of the most important things to remember is that your team will need to have the knowledge and skills required to develop and operate an interdependent, cooperative economic business model. Clear vision, communication that is multi-dimensional, a flat organizational structure rather than a hierarchical one, a guiding coalition approach to teamwork, and participants who have sufficient self-confidence to acknowledge what they don't know and accept new learning are critical to success. Proven technical skills that support specific endeavors are also critical. How do we know what is needed? From experience. Time and again we permitted friendships and empathy to drive decisions; each time it was a terrible decision for the health of the business or project.

Key business characteristics in the LLIFE Success-network™ model presented below are comprised of **people, processes, and systems.**

The LLIFE Success-network™ System: People, Processes, Systems

The preceding sections of this book provided a landscape that establishes the need for a vehicle that moves our communities into the Information Age. It tells you what you probably already know; there is an urgent need for change if we want to create communities that provide the kind of environment conducive to the life we wish to live. The environment for which we provide the framework has an awesome potential for creating new wealth. Let us reiterate that ours is not a Networking Marketing model, although we understand that there could be sectors of the business that contribute to individual wealth.

In early 2004, Dr. Higginbotham developed his **LLIFE Success-networking™ System.** It was based on his experience while working with another networked organization, but had far fewer attributes than the one he ultimately developed. His Success-networking™ model not only differs from the go-it-alone pathway to success that rarely works, according to statistics on start-up business failures. His business model is based upon an effectively performing group of people strategically organized for successful outcomes.

This section of the book provides a step-by-step blueprint that you can follow to establish your own success-networking community.

People, processes, and systems are the components of our model. People are at the core, because they drive the need, and are best able to find viable solutions to problems.

Processes provide the blueprint for change. The processes are 1) the foundation and 2) success-networking.

People

People are the cornerstone of any endeavor. Even if you operate in a technical support area, the behavior of the people charged with carrying out the operation will greatly impact your capacity for success. Selection of the people who impact others on your team must be done with great care.

You've probably experienced the customer service agent from hell, or the totally incompetent technician. What about the revolving instructions you get from a service provider that changes depending on the time of day you contact them? Whoever selected these people either did not care or was unaware of the chaos they were creating. Clearly the selection or training failed.

The most frequently overlooked parts of any new endeavor are the spirit and readiness of the people who will spearhead the initiative. If an organization's people do not have clarity about the mission, and do not have the requisite skills to manage the process and systems, the endeavor will suffer. If the core people do not have a very strong sense of their own value, they will find it difficult to see value in others except from a status perspective.

When asked why they consistently perform better than their competitors, Southwest Airlines management always sites its hiring philosophy: hire for attitude and train for skill. Although people who are members of an organization are not considered to be hired, you do need to consider attitude when selecting a subset of your organization to take an active role in success-networking.

Select the kind of people that best align with the purpose, goals, and objectives of the group. If the purpose of the group is to form a winning golf team, then you must enlist those members who play the game skillfully and who have a stated desire to win. You don't want to carry dead weight. And, there are personal characteristics to consider for the enhancement of unity between the members of the group.

Selection

Desired Behaviors of People Selected for Key Roles

Our experience is that the success of any endeavor rises or falls on the spirit and capabilities of the people who are responsible. Although there are many resources that advise on behaviors that support success, including the Bible, we have found that Don Miguel Ruiz's *The Four Agreements* uses a language that most can easily understand. *The Four Agreements* exposes self-limiting beliefs and presents a simple yet effective code of personal conduct learned from his Toltec ancestors. Basically, it presents a picture of unconditional human faith.

We urge organizations or persons seeking to form interdependent alliances to seek people with the following characteristics. These descriptions are taken from *The Four Agreements*.

1. **Be Impeccable with Your Word**

   Speak with integrity. Say only what you mean. Avoid using words to speak against yourself or to gossip about others. Use the power of your words in the direction of truth and love.

Impeccable means "without sin" and a sin is something you do or believe that goes against yourself. It means not speaking against yourself, to yourself or to others. It means not rejecting yourself. To be impeccable means to take responsibility for yourself, to not participate in "the blame game."

Regarding words, the rules of "action-reaction" apply. What you put out will return to you. Proper use of words creates proper use of energy, putting out love and gratitude perpetuates the same in the universe. The converse is also true.

Impeccability starts at home. Be impeccable with yourself and that will reflect in your life and your relationship with others. This agreement can help change thousands of other agreements, especially ones that create fear instead of love.

2. **Don't Take Anything Personally**

Nothing others do is because of you. What others say and do is a projection of their own dream. When you are immune to the opinions and actions of others, you won't be the victim of needless suffering.

If you don't agree with what others say about you, their words will not affect you emotionally. If you don't care about what others think about you, their words or behavior cannot affect you.

Even if someone yells at you, gossips about you, harms you or yours, it still is not about you! Their actions and words are based on what they believe in their personal dream.

People's personal "Book of Law" and belief system makes them feel safe. When people have beliefs that are different from your own, you get scared, defend yourself, and impose your point of view on others. If someone gets angry with you, it is because your belief system is challenging theirs, and they get scared. They need to defend their point of view. Why become angry, create conflict, and expend energy arguing when you are aware of this?

3. **Don't Make Assumptions**

Find the courage to ask questions and to express what you really want. Communicate with others as clearly as you can to avoid misunderstandings, sadness, and drama. With just this one agreement, you can completely transform your life.

When we make assumptions it is because we believe we know what others are thinking and feeling. We believe we know their point of view, their dream. We forget that our beliefs are just our point of view based on our belief system and personal experiences and have nothing to do with what others think and feel.

We make the assumption that everybody judges us, abuses us, victimizes us, and blames us the way we do ourselves. As a result we reject ourselves before others have the chance to reject us. When we think this way, it becomes difficult to be ourselves in the world.

Take action and be clear to others about what you want or do not want; do not gossip and make assumptions about things others tell you. Respect other points of view and avoid arguing just to be right. Respect yourself and be honest with yourself. Stop expecting the people around you to know what is in your head.

4. **Always Do Your Best**

Your best is going to change from moment to moment; it will be different when you are healthy as opposed to sick. Under any circumstance, simply do your best and you will avoid self-judgment, self-abuse, and regret.

Doing your best means enjoying the action without expecting a reward. The pleasure comes from doing what you like in life and having fun, not from how much you get paid. Enjoy the path traveled and the destination will take care of itself.

Living in the moment and releasing the past helps you to do the best you can in the moment. It allows you to be fully alive right now, enjoying what is present, not worrying about the past or the future.

Have patience with yourself. Take action. Practice forgiveness. If you do your best always, transformation will happen as a matter of course.

Although it is time consuming to select the right people, doing so will eliminate problems later. People who exhibit the characteristics listed above will be resilient. Their diligence and perspective will help make your organization more successful than you imagined.

Process & Systems

Without a clearly defined process, chaos will be the order of the day. Each person is free to "make it up as they go along." Organizations seldom survive such chaos.

Unfortunately, people who own the process never figure out that their lack of a clearly defined process was the cause of its failure. Providing attention to this detail on the front end will eliminate heartbreak later.

Essential components of a Success-networking™ organization

There are seven essential components of a success-networking organization: *training; unifying principles; communication; organization; the plan; commitment; and, action.* Training is the glue that holds everything else together, and is covered in the section immediately preceding this one.

The objective of a success-networking organization is to achieve a state of unity within the group as well as a state of unity between the group and its universe. Unity within networking is a genuine state of caring and sharing, a state that transcends the individual differences of race, religion, politics, education, and our weaknesses. When the condition of unity is reached within the network, *Success- networking™ is achieved.*

1. Training: preparation for success

It is grossly unfair to place people in a position of responsibility without ensuring that they are prepared for success. Each success group will have different learning needs; therefore learning content will be highly customized to ensure success. When selection is done carefully, a team will have the capability and desire to learn.

There are basics that team members must learn in order to support the team's goals. This will not change with the group's focus. Rather, specific, topical training will be in addition to basic Preparation for Success training. Refer to this book's **Section I: LEARNING: CORNERSTONE OF A SUCCESS PROJECT** for a specific plan to ensure that your team is engaged in learning. This section also shows you exactly how to ensure that learning is strategic.

2. Unifying Principles

Unifying Principles are one's highest priorities or values in life. In a networking sense, they become the glue that molds the success group into a performing entity. In its most fundamental form, a unifying principle is an idea that has stood the test of time. It is a generalization of truth used as a basis for goal planning and as a guide for daily living – an idea considered of real worth. Examples of unifying principles are:

- *Commitment to a better way*
- *A belief in people*

- *Personal Integrity*
- *Intellectual Growth*
- *Principled Behavior*

3. Communication

Communication is the third essential component to *Success-networking*™. Without proper communication channels and continuous communication flow, groups and organizations become diseased, stagnant, and eventually perish.

Communication is the lifeblood of any organization. If we are to achieve unity, we must learn to communicate honestly with each other, going deeper than the façade of our masks, and developing a significant commitment to "rejoice together", "mourn together", and to "delight in each other", making the conditions of others our own.

4. Organization

Organization is the fourth essential component to *Success-networking*™. What does the network look like, sound like, etc.? How does it come together, when does it come together, and why does it come together? Obviously, there are many considerations encountered when one undertakes the task of creating a *Success Group*™ *(SG)*.

The *Success Group* is a "free/private enterprise" model designed to guarantee public participation in the basic socioeconomic decisions that affect our daily lives in the workplace, in the neighborhood, and in the marketplace. It subscribes to a "collaborative imperative." In other words, structured collaborations are essential to its existence. Decisions should be made in the public interest, not in the special interest of big business.

In order to compete, we must unite and become strong economically as well as politically. The SG is an incredible vehicle through which to unite and begin to participate in the problem solving process.

The following considerations established the development of the *Success Group* concept.

Motivation: The *SG* is motivated by its stated purpose: the economic survival of its members and the need for public representation.

Size: The size of the organization is critical; therefore great care should be given to it.

Organization: The *SG* is a grassroots concept, is uniquely capitalized, and has a sound structure that supports its goals. It utilizes horizontal links to expand its influence, while creating a strong economic base for unique business acquisitions.

Strategy: Networking with other *SGs* creates a strong economic base for unique business acquisitions and real property investments.

Return on Investment: In addition to the potential monetary return, the *SG* system promises such benefits as knowledge, wellness, public representation, employment, and affordable home ownership.

The *SG* offers a legitimate opportunity to invest in the untapped resources and the entrepreneurial spirit of the American people. Through greater participation in the social, political and economic processes at the grassroots level, a more equitable form of government for and by the people can be created.

5. Plan

The Plan is the fifth essential component to *Success-networking*™. Without a plan, an organization will drift aimlessly and flounder like a ship without a rudder. Although organizations are encouraged to develop their own plan, we use the **Life Build System™**, a plan with the objective of freedom, wellness, and financial security for each member of the Success Group™; and the steps to achieve the objectives, namely teamwork, knowledge, and ownership. The **Life Build System™** – a concentrated educational program – identifies the skills, knowledge, processes critical to success, and attitudes that support success and long term survival of the group. It serves as a pathway to achieving the ultimate in *Success networking*™. Each subject is sequentially planned for the maximum growth and development of the individual and was designed to include and reinforce each component that is essential to success. Some of its exciting components are: *learning, income production, shared equity, social action, and political action.*

6. Commitment

Commitment is the sixth essential component to *Success-networking*™. Without the commitment of the members, the plan will not succeed and the group will eventually perish. There must be a commitment of time, energy, and money to the success of the plan. The rewards to such a commitment are substantial, possibly beyond your wildest belief.

7. **Action**

Action is the seventh essential component to *Success-networking*™. Without action, the group cannot survive. Many plans have been drawn by individuals and organizations, and commitments to those plans have been promised. However, without action, the state of inertia will reduce the group to a shell.

The system of our model *Success-networking*™ operation is comprised of three units: **Success Organization, Success Group, and Success Team.**

The Success Organization™

The *Success Organization* represents the *total* membership. It is divided into *Success Groups* for communication and organizational purposes. These groups are divided into *Success Teams*. It is **highly recommended** that all *Success Groups*, although autonomous, and all *Success Teams* adhere to the same dimensions and same functions.

Success Group™

Since your participation in a *Success Group* is the key to your achieving the life you envision for yourself and your family, it is imperative that you absorb all there is to know and experience about this new thing called a *Success Group*.

The following activities represent a list of suggested considerations for building your *Success Group*.

1. **Success Group Purpose:** Determine the reason for the building of the group. It is the glue that binds the membership. As previously discussed, the purpose establishes the basis for a strongly motivated group, when <u>*positive*</u> in its intent. Examples of a positive purpose are the improvement of the members, their families, their communities, and/or society as a whole.

2. **Success Group Goals and Objectives:** Narrow the purpose into a stated and written action form. They should answer the questions of what you're going to do and how you're going to do it. They are the targets to strive for, as well as the rudder that steers the ship. The *goals and objectives* must be consistent with the groups' unifying principles.

3. **Personal Criteria:** Select the kind of people that best align with the purpose, goals, and objectives of the group. As stated earlier, if the purpose of the group is to form a winning golf team, then you must enlist those members who play the game skillfully and who have a stated desire to win. You don't want to carry dead weight. And, there are personal characteristics to consider for the enhancement of unity between the members of the group.

4. **Unifying Principles:** The establishment of principles creates the grid through which all decisions and all actions of the *Success Group* are determined. The members of the *Success Group* should engage in an activity to establish the group's unifying principles. The principles will determine the group's quality of life and its duration of life. This step is essential; it was made as one of the primary components of *Success-networking™*.

5. **Group Size:** The size of the group should be determined by the number of people required to achieve the purpose, goals, and objectives of the group.

   The size should be large enough to have impact, yet small enough to be managed. It should also enable the organization to acknowledge and empower each individual.

6. **Membership Acquisition Message and Strategy:** Create a written plan as to who, how, and when the potential candidates will be enrolled into the group. The plan becomes your road map toward the most efficient accomplishment of the desired group enrollment.

7. **Membership Building Incentives and Bonuses:** Depending upon the total size requirement of the organization and the criteria for membership, there may be an opportunity to reward those who are the most active and the most effective at enabling the organization to reach its desired membership goals. However, if the establishment of the success

organization has incorporated the foundation as prescribed herein, the moral cause and the enhancement of humankind will suffice as incentive and bonus for those who participate in the organization's development.

How a group unites its members and the extent to which it accomplishes its goals and objectives is often determined by its form and scope of the organization. There are several factors that must be considered in order to establish an effective and efficiently operating *Success Group*.

8. **Success Group Communications:** The blood of any organization or group is its method and frequency of communication with its membership. Unlike hierarchical structured groups, the *Success Group* concept enables a rapid flow of communication from top to bottom, bottom to top, and sideways. There are many forms of communication. All forms should be utilized and should be selected on the requirements of the information and the needs of the users.

9. **Agreements and By-laws:** The order and behavior of a *Success Group* is determined by the agreements and by-laws established between its members. This step outlines the rights and privileges of the individual members of the group, as well as the process for their decision-making. Since the *Success Group* is one of similar groups within the success organization, the same agreements and by-laws become the code for the interaction between all groups.

10. **Organizing Requirements:** The *Success Group* is organized into teams to carry out the various functions that align with the goals and objectives of the group. The team assignment, when paralleled with assignments of other teams within the *Success Organization*, create both a vertical and horizontal structure for information gathering and income production, as well as channels for organizational communication and decision-making.

    Tasks and activities, as well as creating a calendar, should be defined and written in order to facilitate cross-team participation and group monitoring.

    The *Success Group* is multi-dimensional in its organization and purpose. It is established to address the multiple problems within the community, as well as the political and economic growth and development of its members. Therefore, the considerations for its activation must be multi-dimensional and innovative.

11. **Organizational Forms:** The ability of the group to interact as a separate and distinct entity for its optimum political and economic advantage is often determined by its legally represented form. The organizational form can also determine the liabilities of the group, its members, and their assets. There are many different legal forms to consider – association, Limited Liability Company, LLC partnership, corporation, trust, foundation, for profit, non-profit, etc.

12. **Power of Contracts:** Capitalization of the *Success Group* is an important step in the activating process. It

establishes the group's opportunity to participate in the business world as an economic entity. Even when the group's members are financially able to create substantial initial capitalization, the utilization of contracts will add a compounding effect.

13. **Limited Liability Company:** Similar to the cooperative partnerships, the limited liability company agreement unites the *Success Groups* within the *Success Organization* for joint ownership of designated income-producing projects.

Success Teams™

Business Team Concept: When the *Success Group* organizes itself into *Success Teams*, those teams can be assigned the primary functions normally found in any business, e.g., sales, finance, administration, and distribution. Once organized in this fashion, the *Success Group* is positioned to market a product of their choosing for income production. Since all of the *Success Groups* have the same alignment, the *Success Organization* is in a very strategic position for choosing and marketing a product.

Social and Political Action: By designating a social action team and a political action team, the *Success Group* has positioned itself to make a positive contribution to its community and to inform its members of their political empowerment. This opportunity is compounded since all of the *Success Groups* have the same organizational alignment and are able to concentrate more people effort synergistically to accomplish the community and political objectives of the *Success Organization*.

Other: 21st century communication tools such as social media, mobile communications, on-line conference and training, and shared project management platforms make it feasible for people to efficiently conduct social-networking business. Specific tools will depend on the characteristics of the group.

Moments of Contemplation

The realization of ignorance is the first act of knowing.
Jean Toomer, Essentials, 1931

SECTION VI:
FINAL THOUGHTS

We leave you with information about the value of networks, from Jessica Lipnack and Jeffrey Stamp. In their 1982 book, *Networking,* they identified seven categories under which networks are forming because people perceive another way of meeting their needs and of organizing the country. Reasons given are as follows, with categories in parenthesis:

Healing (health and life cycle) networks have formed because people want to be well.

Sharing (communities and cooperatives) networks have formed because people are happiest when they are actively working within their communities, whether geographic or conceptual.

Using (ecology and energy) networks have formed because people want to benefit from the earth's bounty without harming it.

Valuing (politics and economics) networks have formed because people want sane politics and a fair economic system.

Learning (education and communications) networks have formed because people want to learn and they want to communicate – two interrelated human drives.

Growing *(personal and spiritual growth)* networks have formed because people quest for inner peace and for understanding of the nature of the universe.

Evolving *(global and futures)* networks have formed because people have come to understand that nationalism, limitless growth, and political hegemony are antiquated ideas that ignore the reality that we are 7 billion still-primitive people living on a tiny percent of the surface area of one small planet in one remote solar system of billions of galaxies dancing through space.

Perhaps you have been able to glean the reasons why you should begin, right now, to work together systematically. It is critical to our very survival. You should also have a good idea about the process of making it happen. Certainly, you have become more aware of the potential disaster that lies ahead on the well-traveled Industrial Age road. And, perhaps you have also become more aware of the potential golden opportunities that lie ahead on the road to the New Information Society.

The vision for living that we described in the **INTRODUCTION** section of this book can become a reality through our Success-networking™ system, or by following a system of your own. Remember, this is neither an overnight nor a 30-day process. Anything of lasting value never is. Relationships must be solidified, skills assessed and possibly acquired, and knowledge learned. But the end result is well worth the time and effort, and lasts throughout generations.

SECTION VII:
LESSONS LEARNED IN THE FIELD

When we first set out to write *Collaborations, Teamwork, and Networking*, we were hopeful that it could begin to convince people to experience working collaboratively to change their communities for the better. Perhaps an honest description of our hopes is naiveté. After all, change is frightening, even change for the better. This 2nd edition of our book incorporates the lessons we learned as we worked with groups to incorporate the Success-networking™ system across the U.S.

Failures

We discovered that the adage "failures are the best teachers" is absolutely correct.

We were delighted to see the eagerness with which our premise was originally received. Feedback indicated that people could readily see the value of the system we described. However, the adage of "the devil is in the details" proved yet again to be true. Eagerness, in our experience, proved to be an obstacle rather than an asset. The process appears to be simple; this led people to believe that they were ready to embrace business and community-building without adequate preparation. Unfortunately, without new learning and unlearning old habits, they could not understand the power of existing belief systems that thwarted their good intentions. For instance, if a culture of distrust and exclusion existed, it was impossible to embrace a belief that people from different families, church organizations, or zip codes could find a common vision and work collaboratively to attain it. If people had no experience working with successful teams, the concept of effective teamwork had little meaning. If participants did not have a sense of their own potential as well as the impact of areas outside the scope of their capabilities, efforts were easily derailed.

The relatively simple processes we endorse require targeted training in order to develop core capabilities necessary to support creating effective teams, capable leaders, and systems capable of monitoring performance and milestones. Systems created to serve the Industrial Age must be replaced with Information Age systems. Equally important is creating relationships with others who share the belief that they are empowered to change their own community, and also share a vision of what the improved community can be. Trust and vision must be established.

Successes

Despite the lack of adequate preparation, groups that embraced our system were successful in developing frameworks for businesses that employed people within their community. As could be expected, efforts have been hampered without adequate preparation.

We launched a Success Group™ in an urban area that is known for its high crime rate and lack of resources. Despite the surroundings, the group was able to work in a limited collaborative way to establish a Farmers Market and a soul food restaurant. Because we are community owned, we were able to support hiring from within our community. To this end we gave second chances to deserving, hard-working people who would otherwise have been excluded from an opportunity for employment. We have been able to provide on-the-job training opportunities for young people who might not have otherwise had access to such experiences. Economics in the area caused us to suspend our projects; however, despite the difficulties, we count these small milestones as successes.

More information about these endeavors can be found online at www.eslfarmersmarket.com and www.soulfoodcafe-esl.com.

Moving Forward

We are even more committed to sharing our vision throughout the United States and beyond. In a recent CNN documentary *Blacks in America*, Reverend DeForest Soaries, who has created a program designed to liberate the 7,000-member congregation of First Baptist Church of Lincoln Gardens, N.J. from debt, calls debt "the new slavery." Unemployment is at a critically high rate. We are energized by the efforts of people such as Reverend Soaries, and look to learn from his experiences. Programs such as his validate our belief that we all have to take a more proactive role in looking after our own. We are our own helping hands.

Based on our experience, we need to do several things in preparation for embracing a community-building concept that has proven viable in numerous other cultures and countries. We call this foundation work critical to creating Success-networks™ V-CAT (Vision, Capabilities, Accountabilities, and Trust). A broadened list of needed activities includes:

1. Establish and communicate a shared vision - continuously
2. Prepare for leadership – Establish capabilities, including skills, knowledge, and other resources
3. Build accountabilities into the system (What gets measured gets done)
4. Build trust within the organization or community you serve
5. Find areas of agreement
6. Dial back on the tendency to exclude people who are not carbon copies of ourselves
7. Dial back on the tendency to exclude people who do not behave as if they are subordinate to you
8. Relinquish the need to "control" people. Embrace true shared ownership
9. Temper the need for personal gain in favor of the greater good

Lessons learned during our experience have enabled us to develop targeted learning modules that build specific capabilities that have multiple practical applications. We have integrated learning that helps our students get in touch with their core strengths and develop a sense of purpose. We don't assume that Information Age systems are automatically known and embraced. To this end, we insist that our students experience Financial Intelligence Training, information that teaches students to adopt a mindset of a prosumer – a producer and consumer of goods and services. We embed an awareness of how to build wealth, using contemporary financial instruments. We also stress responsibility for self, as well as the community. Leadership Intelligence Training focuses on developing capabilities for effective leaders who inspire confidence and trust.

Moments of Contemplation

Your thought life controls your daily life.
Dr. Gerald's Teachings

When you flee temptation, don't leave a forwarding address.
Based on a quote by Lane Olinghouse

If we must have justice, we must be strong; if we must be strong, we must come together; if we must come together, we can only do so through the system of organization.
Marcus Garvey

Organize as a group ... those who realized the strength of their cultural group, their political demands were considered and determined by the force of their cultural grouping.
Claude McKay

Pick your friends but not to pieces.
Author Unknown

About the Authors

Gerald A. Higginbotham (Dr. G)

Gerald (Dr. G) Higginbotham is Executive Director of Unity for a Better Community. He is an educator, entrepreneur, and community activist who is also an airline pilot of 24 years. He holds a certificate from the Joseph School of Business and Entrepreneurship, and diplomas from Light Bible College and Power Learning Systems in Information Age Development. He also holds a BA in Psychology from California State University, Northridge and a Ph.D. in Biblical Studies and Divinity from the Jesus of Nazareth Church Ministries.

Gerald has a long history of business development and community activism. In 1991 he developed a network of entrepreneurs who implemented and operated a successful restaurant in the St. Louis area. He was instrumental in introducing Financial Literacy education to numerous faith-based organizations, and co-founded a successful wellness center in the Atlanta area.

Gerald is currently CEO and President of Living Learning in Faith Everyday, Inc. (LLIFE), and Executive Director of Unity For A Better Community, Inc., a 501.(3)(c) Organization.

Joyce Coleman

Joyce Coleman is a speaker and management consultant in the areas of customer-focused enterprise and peak performance. She has developed and implemented immensely successful programs for a fortune 500 company, universities, and other organizations. Her work has consistently resulted in improved service, lower costs, and greater satisfaction among customers and employees.

Joyce is also author of the critically acclaimed memoir, *Soul Stirrings: How looking back gives each of us the freedom to move forward,* a companion Study Guide for grades 4-12, and numerous electronic books. She has authored many business-oriented writings that are published widely on the Internet. Joyce helps her clients leverage their intellectual resources to achieve their

goals. She is the president of an online publishing company. Visit her at www.locusthillpublishing.com, and at
www. Joycecoleman.com.

Bibliography

Anderson, Claud. *Black Labor White Wealth.* Englewood, CO: Duncan & Duncan. 1994.

Buckingham, Marcus and Clifton, Donald O. *Now, Discover Your Strengths.* New York: Simon & Schuster Books. 2001.

Covey, Stephen. *The 7 Habits of Highly Effective People.* New York: Fireside. 2000.

Fraser, George C. *Success Runs in Our Race.* New York: William Morrow & Company, Inc. 1994.

Hansen, Mark Victor and Allen, Robert G. *Cracking the Millionaire Code.* Harmony. 2005.

Hill, Napoleon. *The Law of Success.* Northbrook, IL: Success Unlimited. 1979.

Keiersey, David and Bates, Marilyn. *Please Understand Me.* Delmar, CA: Prometheus Nemesis Book Company. 1984.

Kiyosaki, Robert. *Rich Dad Poor Dad.* New York: Warner Books. 2004.

Lipnack, Jessica and Stamps, Jeffrey. *The Age of The Network.* Oliver Wight Ltd. 1994.

Lindo, Ernest. *It's Our Time.*

Maxwell, John. *Your Roadmap for Success.* Thomas Nelson. 2002.

Mother Jones Magazine. May 2005 issue.

Naisbitt, John. *Megatrends.* Warner Books. 1980.

Ruiz, Don Miguel. *The Four Agreements.* Amber-Allen Publishing. 1997.

Scott, Stephen K. *The Richest Man Who Ever Lived.* Waterbrook Press. 2006.

Toffler, Alvin *The Third Wave.* Bantam   Books. New York: Bantam. 1984.

Toffler, Alvin. *Power Shift.* New York: Bantam Books. 1981.

Toffler, Alvin. *Creating a New Civilization: The Politics of The Third Wave.* Turner Pub. 1995.

Warren, Rick. *The Purpose Driven Life.* Zondervan. 2002.

Hilliard, Ira V. *The Courage To Get To Your Wealthy Place.* Life Change Ministries.

ABC News online.

Liberty International Publishing, Inc. *The Phenomenon-Monopoly Men.*

Resources

INSIGHTS into the African-American experience

Access these papers from this web page:
http://www.llife.org/insights.htm

12 Things The Negro Must Do For Himself by Nannie Helen Burroughs. Free Download.

Plight Deepens for Black Men, Studies Warn By Erik Eckholm. Free Download.

They are Still Our Slaves This is the article Dee Lee read on a New York radio station. Free Download.

The Black Matrix (revised 2009) by Franklin G. Jones. Free Download.

21 Things African-Americans Need to Do, according to Tavis Smiley. Free Download.

Resolution Adopted by the [United Nations] General Assembly64/169. International Year of People of African Descent. Free Download.

Video: Resolution Adopted by the United Nations General Assembly.

Video: Is Debt a Bigger Problem than Racism? From CNN's Blacks in America series narrated by Soledad O'Brien.

Financial Intelligence Training

LLIFE Investment Terms. Bonus Free Download. Get a head start by learning the Language of the Rich.
(http://www.llife.org/llife-Investment-Terms-FinLit.pdf)

Financial Intelligence Training. Download Syllabus of our course that prepares you for business-building and personal financial success.
(http://www.llife.org/Financial_Intelligence_Training.pdf)

Leadership Intelligence Training

Leadership Intelligence Training Tool. Bonus Free Download. This workbook is free to those who purchase the electronic version of *Collaboration, Teamwork, and Networking*. When you complete this exercise you will know exactly the kind of leader you aspire to be, what you hope to accomplish as a leader, and the leader you would like to use as a pattern for your own style. Armed with this intel, your knowledge, understanding, and preparedness will set you apart.
(http://www.llife.org/Leadership-Intelligence-Training-DevelopingLeaderWorkbk.pdf)

Leadership Intelligence Training. Download Syllabus of our course that provides a roadmap for accomplishing three very important things:
(http://www.llife.org/Leadership-Intelligence-Training.pdf)

1. How to work together to create jobs, wealth, and stronger communities.

2. How to work together to re-build communities around a common vision.
3. How organizations and communities can work together to build jobs, wealth, and a desirable living environment.

Email us at info@llife.org for further information